ADULT CHILDREN OF ALCOHOLICS

Published by Health Communications, Inc.
Enterprise Center
3201 S.W. 15th Street
Deerfield Beach, FL 33442

ISBN 0-932194-15-X

ACKNOWLEDGMENTS

I want to thank those many people who helped to make this book possible. They are the children of alcoholic parents of all ages, and the children of non-alcoholic parents of all ages.

To Diane DuCharme, who convinced me to write this book.

To Sue Nobleman, Debby Parsons, Tom Perrin, and Rob, for their tireless devotion to the project.

To Lisa, Danny and Dave.

To Kerry C., Jeff R., Irene G., Eleanor Q., Barbara P., Martha C., Loren S., my students at Montclair State, my students at Rutgers Summer School for Alcohol Studies, my students in the Advanced Techniques in Family Therapy Course (Westchester Council on Alcoholism), Sharon Stone, Harvey Moscowitz, Linda Rudin, Eileen Patterson, Bernard Zweben, and James F. Emmert.

Table of Contents

foreword

ADULT CHILDREN OF ALCOHOLICS was originally written only with children of alcoholics in mind. Since its publication, we have learned that the material discussed applies to other types of dysfunctional families as well. If you did not grow up with alcoholism, but lived, for example, with other compulsive behaviors such as gambling, drug abuse, or overeating, experienced chronic illness, profound religious attitudes, were adopted, lived in foster care, or in other potentially dysfunctional systems, you may find that you identify with the characteristics. It appears that much of what is true for the children of alcoholics is also true for others, and that this understanding can help reduce the isolation of countless persons who also thought they were "different" because of their life experience. Welcome.

Janet G. Woititz

introduction

During the last several years, more and more research has been done on alcoholism in this society. Although figures vary, there is general agreement that there are upwards of ten million alcoholics in this country.

These people, as well as being victims themselves, have an adverse impact on those with whom they associate. Employers, relatives, friends and families of alcoholics suffer from the effects of alcoholism. Many man hours of work are lost because of absenteeism and inefficiency due to alcoholism. Relatives and friends are manipulated into making excuses for and covering up for the alcoholic. The promises of reform, although short-lived, are believed because those who care want to believe them, and, as a result, they unknowingly become part of the disease pattern.

Those who are the closest suffer most of all. The family is affected when the employer has to terminate the alcoholic's services. The family is affected when the relatives and friends can no longer tolerate the consequences of alcoholism and avoid the alcoholic and his/her family. The family is also directly affected by the alcoholic's behavior. Unable, without help, to counteract this, the family members get caught up in the consequences of the illness and become emotionally ill themselves.

The bulk of popular interest has been with alcoholism, alcohol abuse and alcoholics. Less attention has been paid to the family, and, more specifically, to the children living in alcoholic homes.

There is little question that there are large numbers of children affected by living in alcoholic homes. Identification of these children has been difficult for several reasons, including embarrassment, ignorance of alcoholism s a disease, denial, and protection of children from unpleasant realities.

Although the suffering manifests itself behaviorally in different ways, children of alcoholics seem to have in common a low self-esteem. This is not surprising, since the literature indicates that the conditions which lead an individual to value himself and to regard himself as a person of worth can be briefly summarized by the terms "parental warmth," "clearly defined limits," and "respectful treatment."[1]

There is considerable literature in which it is argued that these conditions are absent or inconsistently present in the alcoholic home.[2] The alcoholic parent's behavior is affected by the chemicals within, and the non-alcoholic parent's behavior is affected by reaction to the alcoholic. Little emotional energy remains to consistently fulfill the many needs of children who become victims to the family illness.

Parents are models whether they want to be or not. According to Margaret Cork, it is in the give-and-take of his relationships with his parents and others that the child finds a sense of security, self-esteem and an ability to deal with complex inner problems he is facing.[3]

Coopersmith's study with adolescent boys indicates that children develop self-trust, venturesomeness, and the ability to deal with adversity if they are treated with respect and are provided with well-defined standards of values, demands for competence and guidance toward solutions of problems. The development of individual self-reliance is fostered by a well-structured, demanding environment, rather than by largely unlimited permissiveness and freedom to explore in an unfocused way.

The research of both Stanley Coopersmith and Morris Rosenberg have led them to believe that pupils with high self-esteem perceive themselves as successful. They are relatively free of anxiety and psychosomatic symptoms, and can realistically assess their abilities. They are confident that their efforts will meet with success, while being fully aware of their limitations. Persons with high self-esteem are outgoing, socially successful, and expect to be well received. They accept others and others tend to accept them.

On the other hand, according to Coopersmith and Rosenberg, pupils with low self-esteem are easily discouraged and sometimes depressed. They feel isolated, unloved and unlovable. They seem incapable of expressing themselves or defending their inadequacies. They are so preoccupied with their self-consciousness and anxiety that their capacity for self-fulfillment can easily be destroyed.[4]

My own research into "Self-Esteem in Children of Alcoholics"[5] showed that children of alcoholic parents have lower self-esteem than those who do not come from homes where alcohol is abused. This was expected. Since self-esteem is based most importantly on the amount of respectful, accepting and concerned treatment from significant others, it is logical to assume that the inconsistency of the presence of these conditions in an alcoholic home would negatively influence one's ability to feel good about him or herself.

Interestingly enough, a variable such as the age of the subject was insignificant as a determinant of self-esteem.[6] Eighteen-year-olds and twelve-year-olds saw themselves in essentially the same way. They may behave differently, but they don't have different self feelings. This points up the fact that self-perceptions do not change over time without some form of intervention. The way the self attitude manifests itself will change, but not the self-perception.

If this is true, and research tends to support this concept, then an important population to pay attention to are the ADULT CHILDREN OF ALCOHOLICS.

We have not ignored this population. We have simply not labeled them fully. We have called them alcoholics. We have called them spouses of alcoholics. We have not given them acknowledgment of the full measure of their exposure. It is time to identify them further. It is time to call them alcoholic-ACAP. It is important to recognize this factor, because there are very profound implications for treatment if we do so. The adult child of an alcoholic has been affected and has reacted in ways that those who are not adult children of alcoholics may not have. This book will profile for you the adult child of the alcoholic, what it means, and what the implications are.

It will discuss how poor self-image shows itself, and will offer very specific suggestions as to ways to change, if that is desirable.

I have been working with groups of adult children of alcoholics. We are taking an in-depth look at their thoughts, attitudes, reactions, and feelings, and the powerful influence of alcohol in their lives.

Half of the group members are recovering alcoholics, the other half are not. Half are men. Half are women. The youngest member is 23. Some are married, some single. Some have children, some do not. All are committed to self-growth.

There are certain generalizations that recur in one form or another at virtually every meeting. These perceptions are worthy of careful examination and discussion.

1. Adult children of alcoholics guess at what normal behavior is.
2. Adult children of alcoholics have difficulty following a project through from beginning to end.
3. Adult children of alcoholics lie when it would be just as easy to tell the truth.
4. Adult children of alcoholics judge themselves without mercy.
5. Adult children of alcoholics have difficulty having fun.
6. Adult children of alcoholics take themselves very seriously.
7. Adult children of alcoholics have difficulty with intimate relationships.
8. Adult children of alcoholics overreact to changes over which they have no control.
9. Adult children of alcoholics constantly seek approval and affirmation.
10. Adult children of alcoholics usually feel that they are different from other people.
11. Adult children of alcoholics are super responsible or super irresponsible.
12. Adult children of alcoholics are extremely loyal, even in the face of evidence that the loyalty is undeserved.
13. Adult children of alcoholics are impulsive. They tend to lock themselves into a course of action without giving serious consideration to alternative behaviors or possible consequences. This impulsivity leads to confusion, self-loathing, and loss of control over their environment. In addition, they spend an excessive amount of energy cleaning up the mess.

This book is written to and for adult children of alcoholics. It is also my hope that counselors and other interested persons will find it to be of value.

It can be useful in a number of ways: (1) To gain greater knowledge and understanding of what it means to be the child of an alcoholic, and how this process evolves over time; (2) To use as a self-help or clinical guide in working toward individual growth; and (3) As a basis for discussion groups of Adult Children of Alcoholics.

I have had many requests from all over the country as to how to go about setting up groups for adult children of alcoholics, how to meet their special needs, and yet remain true to the principles of AA and Al-Anon. This book provides an answer to these questions.

REFERENCES

[1]Coopersmith, S., "Self-Concept Research Implications for Education." Paper presented to the American Education Research Association, Los Angeles, CA, February 6, 1969.

[2]Bailey, M.B. *Alcoholism and Family Casework.* New York: National Council on Alcoholism, New York City Affiliate Inc., 1968. Hecht, M. "Children of Alcoholics Are Children at Risk," *American Journal of Nursing* 73(10), October 1973: 1764-1767.

[3]Cork, Margaret. *The Forgotten Children.* Toronto, Alcohol and Drug Addiction Research Foundation, 1969, p. 36.

[4]Coopersmith, S. *Antecedents*; Rosenberg, Morris, *Society and the Adolescent Self-Image.* Princeton, New Jersey: Princeton University Press, 1965.

[5]Woititz, J. Doctoral Dissertation, New Brunswick, New Jersey: May, 1976.

[6]Variables such as sex, religion, occupation, and sibling order also proved to have no statistical significance.

1

what happened to you as a child?

When is a child not a child? When the child lives with alcoholism. But, more correctly, when is a child not childlike? You certainly looked like a child, and dressed like a child. Other people saw you as a child, unless they got close enough to that edge of sadness in your eyes or that worried look on your brow. You behaved much like a child, but you were not really frolicking, you were more just going along. You didn't have the same spontaneity that the other kids had. But no one really noticed that. That is, unless they got very close, and even if they did, they probably didn't understand what it meant.

Whatever others saw and said, the fact remains that you didn't really feel like a child. You didn't even have a sense of what it's like to have a child's feelings. A child is very much like a puppy ... offering and receiving love freely and easily, scampering, somewhat mischevious, playful, doing work for approval or a reward, but doing as little as possible. Most important, being *carefree*. If a child is like a puppy, you were not a child.

Others could describe you in a very simple sentence, probably related to the role you adopted in the family. Children who live in alcoholic homes take on roles similar to those taken on in other dysfunctional families. But in this kind of family, we see it very clearly. Others are aware of it, too, only they don't recognize it for what it is.

For example, "Look at Emily, isn't she remarkable? She's the most responsible child I have ever seen. I wish I had one like that at home." If you were Emily, you smiled, felt good, and enjoyed getting the praise. You probably didn't allow yourself to think, "I wish I could be good enough for them." And you certainly didn't allow yourself to think, "I wish *my* parents thought I was terrific. I wish I could be good enough for them." And you certainly didn't allow yourself to think, "Well, if I didn't do it, who would?"

To an outsider looking in, you were simply a remarkable little child. And the truth of the matter is, you were. They just didn't see the whole picture.

You might have taken on another role in the family. You might have been the scapegoat, the one in trouble all the time. You were the family's way of not looking at what was really happening. People said, "Would you look at that Tommy, he's always in trouble. Boys will be boys. I was the same way when I was his age."

If you were Tommy, what did you feel? You might not allow yourself to feel. You'd just look at the person and you'd know that they really *weren't* like you when they were your age. If they were, they wouldn't be so flip about it. Yet, you couldn't allow yourself to say, and probably wouldn't even allow yourself to wonder, "What do I have to do in order to get them to pay attention to me? Why does it have to be this way?"

You might have been more like Barbara and become the class clown. "Gee, she should really be a comedian when she grows up. How clever, how funny, how witty!" And if you were Barbara, you might smile, but underneath you wondered, "Do they know how I really feel? Life really isn't that funny. I seem to have fooled them. I can't let them know."

And then there's little Margaret, or is it Joan? Somehow I can never really get the name straight. That little child off in the corner. That withdrawn child—the one who never gives anyone any trouble. And the little child wonders, "Am I invisible?" That child doesn't really want to be invisible, but hides in a shell, hoping to be noticed, powerless to do anything about it.

You looked like a child, you dressed like a child, to some degree you behaved like a child, but you sure as hell didn't feel like a child. Let's take a look at what it was like at home.

Home Life

Children of alcoholics grow up in similar environments. The cast of characters may be different, but what happens in each alcoholic home is not a whole lot different. The specific happenings may vary but, in general, one alcoholic home environment is like another. The undercurrent of tension and anxiety is ever present. What happens with it in particular may vary, but the resulting pain and remorse predictably follow. The differences exist more in the way you reacted to your experiences than to the experiences themselves.

You internalized what happened differently and, as a result, behaved differently. But most of you felt pretty much the same inside.

Remember what it was like at home? You can visualize what it looked like, but do you remember what it felt like? What did you expect when you walked in the door? You hoped that everything would be fine, but you never really knew for sure. The only thing you were sure of was that you never knew what you would find, or what was going to happen. And somehow, no matter how many times things went awry, as soon as you walked in the door, you were never prepared.

If your father was the alcoholic, sometimes he was loving and warm. He was everything you wanted a father to be: caring, interested, involved, promising all the things that a child wants. And you knew he loved you too.

But other times he wasn't that way. Those were the times he was drunk. When he didn't come home at all, you worried and waited. At home, he passed out, got into big fights with your mother, even came at you, which was really scary. Sometimes you got in the middle, trying to keep the peace. Never knowing what was going to happen, you always felt somewhat desperate. And then the drunk father forgot all those promises he made the day before. That felt strange, because you knew he meant it when he promised them. You thought, "Why doesn't it ever happen? Why doesn't he ever do what he says he is going to do? It really isn't fair."

And then there was your mother. In a very funny kind of way, even with all of his problems, you may have preferred your father. Because she was grouchy and irritable, acting as if she had the weight of the world upon her shoulders, and tired all the time, you felt like you were in the way. Even though she told you that you were not in the way, you couldn't help feeling it.

She may have gone off to work. Your father may not have had a job. You couldn't help feeling that if you weren't in the picture, there wouldn't be all this trouble. Your mother wouldn't be fighting with your father. She wouldn't be tense all the time; she wouldn't be screaming; she wouldn't be so short-tempered. Life could be a whole lot easier if you simply weren't there. And you felt very guilty. Somehow your very existence caused this: if you were a better kid, there would be fewer problems. It was all your fault, but there didn't seem to be anything you could do to make life better.

If your mother was the alcoholic, chances are your father had already left, or was staying pretty late at the office. He didn't want to be around. Or perhaps he came home at lunchtime to do your mother's work. He sewed the buttons on your clothes and made your lunch. That may have happened for a while. But you felt peculiar about it, because you knew it wasn't his job, and he was doing it to make up for the fact that your mother was drunk.

In the end, you probably took over the things that mothers usually do. You learned pretty fast how to cook, clean, and shop. In addition to taking over the care of younger brothers and sisters, in a very real way you may have become a mother to your mother. You may have helped her to eat and clean herself up, even helped her up to bed so the younger kids wouldn't see her passed out. You took care of the whole family.

In her sober moments, your mother tried to make up for what she lacked, and guilt overwhelmed you. There might have been long periods of time when she delayed her drinking to try and keep the home in order. How painful for you to be aware of her struggle. How grateful, but how guilty, you felt as you got more and more confused. Just what was your role?

If both your parents were alcoholic, life was even less predictable, except they took turns getting worse. Being home was like being in hell. The tension was so thick that you could cut it with a knife. That nervous, angry feeling was in the air. Nobody had to say a word, as everybody could feel it. It was extremely tense and uncomfortable. Yet there was no way to get away from it, no place to hide, and you wondered, "Will it ever end?"

You probably had fantasies about leaving home, about running away, about having it over with, about your alcoholic parent becoming sober and life being fine and beautiful. You began to live in a fairy-tale world, with fantasy and in dreams. You lived a lot on hope, because you didn't want to believe what was happening. You knew that you couldn't talk about it with your friends or adults outside your family. Because you believed you had to keep these feelings to yourself, you learned to keep most of your other feelings to yourself. You couldn't let the rest of the world know what was going on in your home. Who would believe you, anyway?

You saw your mother covering up for your father. You heard her making excuses about how he was too sick to go to work. Even if you said something to her about your father, she pretended that it wasn't true. She said, "Oh, nonsense, don't worry about it. Eat your cereal." You learned quickly to keep your father's drinking to yourself, as your stomach churned, you felt tight inside, you cried into the night—if you could still cry.

Your fantasies about leaving home or living with a family that was like the "Brady Bunch," you knew would never happen. It was very difficult for you to go away from home, not even for a weekend. If you left overnight, you worried about what was going on at home: "If I am away from home, I am like a rat leaving a sinking ship. How will they get along without me? They need me." In a very real way, they did need you. Without you, the family would have to relate to each other. There was no escape.

You were trapped. You were trapped physically and trapped emotionally. These feelings are expressed by Gloria in the following dream:

"The following is a description of a dream that I had when I was about eight years old. That was nearly 15 years ago; it remains to date the most vivid and most frightening dream I can remember. It took place during a period of my life when my mother's drinking problem started getting 'serious.'

"The dream was in 'black and white.' A transparent, hazy mist surrounded everything. It was strange to me, because I was not only in the dream, but observing myself in the dream. I could see myself as one might see oneself on TV or film.

"My mother and I were in a very dark and gloomy place; it resembled a dungeon. We were both behind bars in what seemed to be a cage or jail. The place had no walls, no floor, no ceiling; only the cage, my mother and myself, and the black void. I remember pacing back and forth; I was restless, but not frightened. Then, out of nowhere, there appeared a guard, a woman in uniform. She walked up to the cage, unlocked the door, and released my mother. She took my mother by the arm and led her away. I was left behind. And so I waited, patiently, certain that in due time the guard would return and release me also. I waited and waited for what seemed to be an eternity. Finally, something appeared out of the dark. I thought it was the guard coming for me. Instead, it was a strange, inhuman thing, which very slowly passed by the cage and then disappeared out of sight. It vanished into the void, and I was left alone. The thought hit me that no one was going to release me. I was alone. I became panic-stricken.

"I awoke terrified. I was beyond reason. I remember sitting up in bed and screaming. At least, I thought I was screaming. I forced the air from my lungs, but no sound came from my throat. So, I took another huge, deep breath, and still there was no sound. I had lost my voice.

"I was trying to call for my mother. I wanted her beside me so badly, but she had no way of hearing me. So I slid back under the covers and prayed that in the morning my voice would return. And then I went to sleep."

Gloria felt trapped. Gloria was trapped. She was alone with her pain. She told no one, and every day after school she would come straight home and take care of her mother. As painful as that was, it was easier than being at school and worrying. Nobody noticed. Nobody saw. Gloria was a good little girl who did as she was told and gave nobody any trouble.

School

Your home life was not only miserable; it influenced your life at school. How did you do in school? If you were like Emily, the super-achiever and responsible one, you did very well. You were there, doing whatever was asked of you. You got high grades and a lot of praise. You may have even been the kid that got to clean the black-board. And it was an escape for a while, from home and from your true feelings. Nobody thought you were a child with very serious problems. Teachers might have said to your parents, "I wish I had one at home like that."

If you fell into the other categories, your performance was spotty. Depending on how intelligent you were, and how cleverly you had learned to manipulate, you could determine to some extent how well you did in school. You might do well one semester in one course, and badly in another, until finally you gave up all together. Or you slid through. Or, like Don, you tried to bully your way through.

Unfortunately, you took on many characteristics of your alcoholic parent. People behave as they have learned to behave, whether they like it or not—whether they want to or not. Alcoholics do not want to take responsibility for their behavior. Was that you? It certainly was Don.

Don is a 17-year-old high school senior, living with a recovering alcoholic father. His father, during his drinking years, which were most of Don's life, was very argumentative and often violent. He invariably got his own way, because others were afraid of him.

Don came to see me because he was in danger of failing his health class. If he failed, it would mean that he would not graduate. The reason the health teacher gave for his imminent failure was that he had never attended health class.

His first response to the situation was identical to what he had heard his alcoholic father say when he was actively drinking. "He can't do this to me. He has no right to do that. Who does he think he is? I'll report him to the Board of Education. I'll have that bastard's job." And on and on.

I said nothing.

He then tried the tack his father used when he was no longer drinking, but still muddled and still sick. "I know what I'll do. I'll go to his home. I'll throw myself on the ground at his feet. I'll beg. I'll plead. I'll kiss his ring."

With no response from me, he moved to a third phase—one that demonstrated he had worked long and hard on himself. "I guess what I will have to do is make an appointment with him and sit down and see if there is anything I can do to make up the work."

Don had learned to take responsibility for his behavior. It was a hard lesson, because it did not automatically come out of his life experience. Responsibility had to be taught.

If he had remained belligerent, he would have failed and not understood why. He could consider himself a victim and blame others. The child who continues with this behavior becomes more and more anti-social and is likely to end up in a penal institution. Those around him judge his behavior harshly and he will not understand because he did not learn the alternatives.

If he had gotten stuck at the second stage, he might have been able to *pull it off*. The con artist can generally get away with it for a while. This, too, is what he learned at home. The highly manipulative behavior of the alcoholic for a while reaps rewards in terms of achieving the ends that he thinks are desirable. But manipulation doesn't work forever; others stop being fooled and the alcoholic gets caught. This happens to the child of the alcoholic too. He gets away with it—for a while. Having a distorted sense of his own power, he doesn't quite know what hit him when he is finally caught.

The third alternative is the desirable one, as it gave Don the greatest opportunity to resolve his problem in a satisfactory way. It is a way that allowed him to take some pride in himself, no matter what the results. If the teacher will work out a compromise, he will graduate with the class. If the teacher will not work out a compromise, he did what he could to better the situation. He can begin to respect himself.

This particular case has a happy ending. The teacher and Don worked out a program whereby he could make up the work. He was able to graduate with his class.

Another problem in school was the inability to concentrate. Quite often your thoughts were directed to the fantasies you constructed to make life okay, or to worrying. What's going to happen to me? Will everything be all right? What will happen when I get home? You might have gotten into trouble for staring out the window. The teacher said, "Suzy day-dreams all the time. I wish she'd pay better attention."

Well, if you were Suzy, you probably wanted to pay better attention—but how could you? Especially if you had been up all night listening to your parents screaming and yelling at each other. How were you going to concentrate in school if you hadn't had a good night's sleep? And what difference did it make anyway? Things were so bad. Who really cared?. Who really gave a damn if you did well or poorly? If you did well, it wasn't good enough. If you did poorly, you got yelled at. But it passed—nobody really noticed. If you needed help, you knew better than to ask for it. You might get a promise, but nobody had time to help you. So you felt sorry for yourself.

And, if by chance there was someone sympathetic to you, a teacher who said, "Is something wrong, Johnny? You look like there is something bothering you," you automatically said, "No, everything is fine," and walked away, wanting desperately to cling to that teacher, wanting desperately to say, "Oh my God, it's so terrible at home ... I'm not really sure what is wrong, but I know something is wrong. Please, please help me." But you knew that you didn't talk outside the home about what was going on in the home. At the same time, you wished the teacher hadn't let you walk away. You wanted someone to understand without your having to tell them, but you didn't really believe anyone could.

You had learned to keep your feelings to yourself, perhaps not even acknowledging them to yourself. So school, which could have been a haven, became a kind of hell. After a while, you may have misbehaved or stopped going. Maybe, maybe, maybe someone would pay attention. If you got into trouble, you might be pressured into telling the truth.

If you withdrew, you knew you'd be left alone, because you were quiet and didn't cause anyone any trouble. And the more you did this, the more alone you would feel, and the harder it would be to do anything else. Becoming the class clown, a welcome diversion to the students, if not the teacher, worked for a while. You got some attention that way—not the kind you wanted, but at least you weren't ignored.

But if you stopped going to school, if you got into big enough trouble, somebody would surely pay attention. You cried for help in the only way you knew how. And then you would be punished, but at least they would have noticed. So that was what school was like. It was an additional punishment, simply a place you had to be. If you were lucky, it offered you a little relief. But mostly, it was something that you *had to go through.*

Friends

What about friends—other kids your own age? You might have played with them, but somehow you didn't feel you were one of them. As involved as you looked in the game, you always felt a little different. You didn't completely belong, so you always felt like an outsider.

It was difficult to make friends for a couple of reasons. One, because it was hard to believe that people really liked you. After all, you had been told all your life that you were such a crummy kid. And if you hadn't been told in words, you knew it was true, because if it wasn't, your father wouldn't have to drink. And even if someone's good feelings toward you were real, it was a little scary to know that if they got to know you a little better and found out, they wouldn't be your friend.

You probably got to know some kids. But that caused problems, too. How many times could you go over to your friend's house without inviting him to your house? There was always a sense of that dreaded day when your friend would say, "Let's play at your house this afternoon." You could only go to your friend's so often without having to face the inevitable. Maybe it just wasn't worth it to have a friend.

So you might have withdrawn, or you might have behaved in such a way that the kids walked away from you. That way you didn't have to face them at all. But if you took the risk and made a friend, you knew the day of being found out would come.

When a sixteen-year-old girl met the older brother of a girl she had made friends with when she was younger, it brought back a lot of memories. And she wrote him this poem:

"To"
I remember you from long ago,
When I was living in a hell
built especially for children.
The walls of your home
were my only salvation.
I'm sure you were never aware of this, though—
because I never really knew you.
This is why I've always known you,
but you never did me.
I was a lonely, horrified child—
with nowhere to go
and no one to turn to ...
So many years later.
You don't remember knowing me,
but I do you.
I needed to be where you stood—
a place so unlike my own.

That household meant a lot to this little girl. However, the dreaded day came—she had to invite her friend to her house. When she brought her friend home, her father was passed out on the living room floor. Her mother very quicky made up a face-saving lie and said, "Oh, he sleeps on the floor because he has a problem with his back and the doctor told him that would be good for his back." The little girl seemed to accept that, but she never came back again. The risk was real. How hard it was to make friends!

And, as you grew up, it became harder and harder because you reached a point where you simply didn't know how to make friends. "What do I talk to them about? Why would they be interested in me? Why would they like me? I'm not a good person. Why would they want me for a friend?" With all those questions going through your head, how could you feel spontaneous, or free? How could you relate well to other kids?

Even if you wanted to stay after school and play with the other kids, it may have been impossible. You may have had to rush home because of responsibilities like taking care of your little brothers and sisters. You may have been worried that your mother was drunk and you would have to take care of her. You may have worried all day and you had to rush right home to see what had happened. In this strange life, you wanted nothing more than to run away, and yet you had to go back as soon as possible.

But that wasn't your life, your reality. It doesn't make a whole lot of sense when you look at it now, but it was what you knew then. A child goes away for a camp experience. She went to a camp designed for children of alcoholic parents.

When the child returns home, she sits down and writes about what it felt like inside. Because, although she knew how to behave, she brought all of the confusion, and all of the concern of being a child living with alcoholism with her. Nobody saw it, but she shared it with me in the following poem.

C.A.M.P.

I don't want to be here.
I want to go home.
I'm not going to have a good time.
I don't have any friends here
And nobody likes me.

Hey! I just had fun!
And I laughed and smiled,
And I feel pretty happy!
Maybe it won't be so bad after all,
Then, again, I want to go home.

I want to go boating again!

When is it time for lunch?
Can we go on a hike?
I want to go fishing some more!
A campfire!

I don't understand these "meetings!"
Everybody is saying all these horrible things
And I know exactly how they feel!
Do they understand how I feel too?
Hey, let's have another one!
No—they put me to sleep.

I really like my counselors, too.
All of them are really nice.
We do whatever we want
And that's O.K.!

What! We're going home tomorrow?
We just got here, didn't we?
Go away! You make me mad!
You're ugly!
And your mother dresses you funny!
I hate you!

Wow, it's really time to go home.
I don't know how I feel about this.
I hope I can come back next year.
I don't want to go home,
I want to be here!

Well, I guess coming here really doesn't matter after all,
Because you still have to go home
To exactly what you left.

What about your sense of yourself? Did you have high self-esteem? Did you value yourself? Or consider yourself worthy? Did you consider yourself at all?

In order to measure self-esteem, you need a sense of self. Did you have one? I'm not so sure. A child determines who he is by the inputs of the significant people around him. As he gets older, he makes those decisions for himself, or ideally, he should. But initially he finds out who he is by what other people say to him, and he internalizes these messages.

But you got a lot of double messages, things that seemed to contradict each other. You didn't know which part was true, so sometimes you picked one part and sometimes you picked the other part. You were never really sure. Paradoxically, these contradictory messages were probably both true. As a result, your sense of self became somewhat distorted. The messages were not clear. They didn't make a lot of sense. So who you were and whether or not you valued that person was very difficult to determine.

For example, you heard, "I love you, go away." What did that mean? Your mother would say to you, "I love you." You heard and felt those words. But you knew that you were in the way, that she didn't have time for you, that her concerns were not with you, and that you were in her hair. "I love you, go away." How does that make sense? Which part did you believe? If you believed both, you were confused.

If you believed "I love you," and yet had to go away, what did that do? If you believed both parts, what was the implication as you grew up? People who told you they loved you, and yet pushed you away could be extremely desirable.

How about the set of double messages, "You can't do anything right ... I need you!" The perfectionism of the alcoholic criticized whatever you did. You got the "A," you needed the "A+." No matter what happened, it wasn't good enough; there was always a way to find fault. You certainly couldn't believe you were able to do anything right, no matter how hard you tried.

But the other part of the message, "I need you. I can't get along without you," caused you to do a lot of chores around the house. You ended up being, to some degree, the emotional support. Why did they need you if you couldn't do anything right? It didn't make a lot of sense, but you knew it was true, because both of those messages were coming through loud and clear.

Next we come to *the greatest* paradox. "Always tell the truth," and, "I don't want to know." You were told to tell the truth always, because being honest was of value. Moreover, you were told that if something happens and you tell the truth, you will get into less trouble. Remember that one?

You could never be sure about that one, as sometimes it was true and sometimes it wasn't true. "I don't want to know" certainly complicated the issue. Why overburden them? Why overburden an already-overburdened parent? This is a wonderful rationalization for someone who doesn't want to take responsibility. What kid wants to own up to a bad deed, especially when he has a parent who models that behavior?

Why give them more to worry about? That is encouraged, at least covertly. Pretty soon you learned that "Always tell the truth" is something you should tell your kids. But the truth really had very little meaning in your household. You heard your parents lie all the time. You heard your non-alcoholic parent covering up for your alcoholic parent, and that was apparently okay. Also, your alcoholic parent was always making promises and never following through. But he didn't seem to be lying when he made the promise.

What was real and what was unreal got very distorted in your household. So there's not a whole lot in it for you to tell the truth. And what happened for a while is that you started lying automatically. And since you didn't feel that you were lying, because everybody's lying, you didn't feel too guilty about it. You may have even fooled yourself into believing you were protecting your family. "They'll feel a lot better thinking my ride home was late," you thought, rather than saying, "They caught us smoking a joint on the street and brought us to the juvenile center."

"I'll be there for you," and "I give you my word, next time," are another set of double messages. Your parent was always making promises like, "Saturday we will do this. We'll get out of this somehow. Everything will be fine. Don't worry about it. I'll buy you the dress. I'll be home for dinner. I care, I'm interested, let's talk about it sometime." And then these things never happened. All lies!

In the other part of the message, "I give you my word, next time," "well, it didn't work out this time, but it will work out next time," the desire to get points for intent and not for behavior became evident. And what did you do with that? Not now, later! The later never came. So there was a third message in there. "Forget it." You learned how not to want.

We then move into the paradox of, "Everything is fine, don't worry." The other part of the message your parent sent out is, "How can I deal with all of this?" A sense of hopelessness, but telling you not to worry. "Okay, okay, I won't worry." Somehow it didn't work that way.

One other confusing message is a judgment on the alcoholic because he or she is an alcoholic, and a dismissal of unacceptable behavior for the same reason. "John is a drunk," was said with contempt. But then you heard, "Yes, he broke his glass, but he couldn't help it, he was drunk." It made no sense. He could not help being drunk if he was an alcoholic, but it was not okay for him to break the glass.

The behavior of the alcoholic got explained away because of the disease. Nobody was allowed to be upset because he or she didn't mean it.

This double standard had to be confusing. The real message was, "If I am drunk, I can do whatever I want." Not only was alcoholism used as a cop-out for the alcoholic, but you probably learned how to use it as a cop-out for your own behavior. For example, "Tell your teacher you've got family problems and she'll let you get away with not having your work done. It works every time."

Ginger was referred to me because of her own drinking, but it was not long before she made sure that I knew how rotten life was because of her father's alcoholism.

> "He's down on me all the time. He is always on my case."
>
> "Tell me, Ginger, what are you talking about specifically?"
>
> "If I get in after curfew he yells at me. (Ginger, at 15, had a curfew of 1:30 a.m.). If I don't say 'good morning,' he really lets me have it."

My response to her was, "Ginger, I don't drink a whole lot, but in my house your curfew would be 11:00, and I would do more than yell if you got in late. You would also say 'good morning' to me, whether you wanted to or not."

It's easy to see that she was using the alcoholism as an excuse to run amuck. Then, when her father's strong reactions proved how terrible he was, in effect, she had set him up. I was pretty rough on Ginger, telling her exactly what I saw her doing, and what I thought of it. I also acknowledged the real difficulties in her life.

> The following week when she returned, I said, "I was pretty hard on you last week; I'm surprised you came back."
>
> "When I left here last week, I felt terrible, so I knew something must be working," she replied.

Not really wanting to get away with her bad behavior, she felt relief at someone finally calling her on it. Her mother's fear of making a bad situation worse by taking a stand had left Ginger very confused. If the child of the alcoholic, not unlike the alcoholic, is ever to mature, there must be accountability. Part of having a strong sense of self is to be accountable for one's actions. No matter how much we explore motives or lack of motives, we are what we do. We take credit for the good, and we must take credit for the bad. The key is to take responsibility for all of our behavior.

The double messages you received as a child caused you to lose sight of yourself. Where are you in the mix? Who's really concerned with you anyway? Your parents don't seem to be. Even if you don't seem to be, your self-image is confused.

The bottom line is that you know your parents love you. You can't prove it, but you just know it. This fact alone is the reason you can overcome the difficulties of your childhood. It is the critical component that not even alcoholism can destroy. The love may have been distorted, but it was real ... your reality was distorted.

Therefore, your sense of self is distorted. Because of this, there are many aspects of life, many aspects of growing up and living life fully, that you haven't learned. You missed the discussions between parent and child of, "How do I handle this?" And, "What do I do if he says this?" "What do I do with this problem? How can I figure it out?" Your parents were so absorbed in the madness of alcoholism that they had neither the time nor the energy to discuss these problems with you.

So there are a lot of things you are unfamiliar with, things that you simply don't know. Moreover, there are many things that you don't even know you don't know, so you don't even know what questions to ask.

What you do know is that you never really feel that you fit in, and you can't figure out why. Everyone else fits in, and you don't even ask why.

Your childhood feelings, thoughts, experiences and assumptions are carried with you, in one form or another, throughout your life. The adult who doesn't work to change and develop remains tied to his parents and/or spouse, reacts in the workplace the same as he did in school, feels isolated despite the presence of other people, and is afraid to let others know him.

This adult also increases the likelihood that he will become an alcoholic, marry an alcoholic, or both, thereby perpetuating a vicious cycle.

2

what is happening to you now?

The child grows into an adult. We all know what an adult is, until we are asked to define the word. When we begin to search for the answers, we wonder. I cannot define for you what an adult is. You have to define it for yourself. Maybe it's the point in your life when you are where the buck stops. Maybe that's when you become an adult—the time when you are in charge of your life.

For the purposes of this book, we're talking about someone who has grown up, who has reached his or her majority. Then you can wonder, even though you are all grown up, "How adult are you?" What role has your history played in your life? What things about your history have you been able to use to your advantage? What things about your history tend to get in your way? What is your perspective on yourself? How do you really, truly see yourself?

You have a lot of questions, many of which lead to new questions. Because your foundation has been ambiguous, you've always had a lot of questions. You may not even have known what all those questions were, but one thing was clear. You didn't have a lot of answers.

Let's take a look at who you are today. Simply take a look. Try not to make the assumption as you look over these characteristics that they are further proof of how damaged you are. If I know you as well as I think I do, that's exactly what you will do.

This list is not the result of a scientific survey. It is a consensus of statements that adult children of alcoholics have made about themselves. They agreed that these characteristics are part of who they are. They may not all be true for you, or only be true to some degree. This is not an attempt to label you, but if the following discussion does nothing else, it will give you a little understanding of why you react the way you do, of what some of the reasons are for some of the behaviors that you have not been able to understand. It's a way to show you that some of the things that have caused you to wonder about your emotional health are carryovers from your childhood.

They may simply be carryovers from being the child of an alcoholic. The form may have changed, but the substance remains the same. In this context, you can look at these characteristics, begin to explore them, and make an effort to change.

Now, let's just take a look at what these characteristics are, what they mean, and what some of the implications are.

1.   Adult children of alcoholics guess at what normal is.

The significance of this statement cannot be overestimated, as it is their most profound characteristic. Adult children of alcoholics simply have no experience with what is normal. Many of them join A.A. or Al-Anon. I am often amused at what happens when they reach the second step: "Came to believe that a power greater than ourselves could restore us to sanity." They absolutely believe that. It's certainly true. It's certainly significant, and important, and essential to recovery. However, they don't know what sanity is. They look at things that appear to be normal and try to copy them. Yet, what they are copying may or may not be normal, so they're behaving as if they are normal, without having a sound basis for making that decision.

It's very similar to the kinds of feelings homosexuals have before coming out of the closet. Having spent a whole lifetime covering up in order not to be found out, they are suffering from a great deal of confusion. They've spent much of their time guessing at what they would be feeling if they were straight, so that others don't have certain information about them.

I don't find this a lot different with the grown children of alcoholics. Throughout life, to keep others from finding out that they don't know what they're doing, they guess at what is appropriate. They get concerned and confused about things that they believe other people do not get concerned and confused about. They don't have the freedom to ask, so they never know for sure. Even more important, they don't want to look stupid. When people like me make statements such as, "The only stupid questions are the ones that are left unasked," they say nothing out loud. But to themselves, they say, "That's what she thinks! If she only knew ...!"

After all, when you take a look at your history, how could you have any understanding of normalcy? Your home life varied from slightly mad to extremely bizarre.

Since this was the only home life you knew, what others would consider "slightly mad" or "extremely bizarre" were usual to you. If there was a day in there that one could characterize as "normal," it certainly was not typical, and therefore could not have had much meaning.

Beyond your chaotic day-to-day life, part of what you did was live in fantasy. You lived in a world that you created all your own, a world of what life would be like IF ... What your home would be like IF ... The way your parents would relate to each other IF ... The things that would be possible for you IF ... And you structured a whole life based on something that was probably impossible. The unrealistic fantasies about what life would be like if your parent got sober probably helped you survive, but added to your confusion.

You saw the "Brady Bunch" or "Father Knows Best" and assumed that people really lived like that. What did you know? The other homes you went into were different from yours, and your hosts probably put their best foot forward. Even if they didn't, you couldn't have a real sense of what life was really like in someone else's home, because you didn't live there.

Children from more typical homes know that these programs don't show life as it really is. They see it as a fairy tale and either enjoy it or get annoyed by the sweetness and perfection, because they know nobody really lives like that, and everything doesn't ALWAYS work out well in the end.

It becomes very clear that you have no frame of reference for what it is like to be in a normal household. You also have no frame of reference for what is OK to say and to feel. In a more typical situation, one does not have to walk on eggs all the time. One doesn't have to question or repress one's feelings all the time. Because you did, you also became confused. Many things from the past contributed to your having to guess at what normal is.

Not too long ago, a 13-year-old boy was referred to me for counseling. Both of his parents were recovering alcoholics, and both were children of alcoholics. Because the boy was having difficulty in school, the vice principal said that he had serious emotional problems and should go for counseling. Knowing that this couple were children of alcoholics gave me some very important information: they did not know what it was like to be thirteen. I knew that as children of alcoholics, they had not been typical 13-year-olds.

Before I even saw their son, I described to them what it was like to be a 13-year-old growing up in a typical home. They were greatly relieved, because I had described their son. No normal 13-year-old is all that easy to live with. After seeing the boy a couple of times, I was pleasantly suprised to find nothing wrong with him. Yes, he was having difficulty in school. Yes, he was very competitive. Yes, he was having a personality conflict with the vice principal. Yet there was no reason for him to see a therapist. There was nothing wrong with this boy that getting over being thirteen wouldn't cure.

Disruption is not exclusive to the alcoholic family system. So-called "normal" families have their share of ups and downs as well. Children living in "normal" families can have behavior problems and be disrupted emotionally. Some of this is part of growing up, and some of it may mean more serious difficulties. The key is to know the difference, and in the family complicated by alcohol, it is harder to sift things out realistically.

Had the parents not been children of alcoholics, they might have recognized typical adolescent behavior. It is to their credit, certainly, that they cared enough to find out. Yet it was a little sad that they were unable to recognize the very fine job of parenting they were doing ... how they were bringing up a very normal, healthy child, who would have all of the usual and normal crises of growing up. Because of their own histories, they simply did not know what normal was.

That is one example of how being the child of an alcoholic, and having to guess at what normal is, can influence parenting.

The following shows how it can influence a marital relationship.

At the time Beth and James came to see me, James had been recovering in A.A. for 16 years, and Beth had spent the same amount of time in Al-Anon. They were a very devoted couple, who had worked long and hard on themselves individually, on their family relationships, and on their marriage. Beth, who was about to have a hysterectomy, saw this as a very significant milestone in her life. She had spent a lifetime taking care of her husband, six children, and the house.

She wanted to be completely pampered for a while. She wanted her kids to take care of her, and her husband to leave his work if he had to, even though he had just become president of a company. She demanded that he take care of the kids and support her emotionally and physically. That this was to be her time, she made clear, and she wanted everybody to like it.

James was supportive, and was encouraging, but she wasn't quite sure he meant it. When they came in, they were at odds.

I knew that James, as well as being an alcoholic himself, was the adult child of an alcoholic parent. This meant that he had grown up in an environment where he wasn't sure how to feel. He wasn't sure what response to the situation was O.K. He was in turmoil, and I could see that the problem needed to be defined.

So I turned to James, and said, "If I were you, I would be feeling a whole lot of things right now. I would want to be very supportive of my wife, because I care about her a whole lot. I would also be thinking that she was making a very big deal out of this hysterectomy, that women all over the world have hysterectomies, and although it is a major operation, it is rarely, if ever, fatal, and she is really making more of a fuss than necessary. Many of my friends' wives have gone through this operation, and it wasn't as big a deal as Beth is making out of it. If I were you, I would want to be there for her to the degree that I could, but I would be very concerned about cancelling business trips, and leaving the office early when I need to see that things were done there; and with the difficulties I am having at the office, to also have to worry about running the household and taking care of the kids. You know, I'd really consider it a burden on me, and I would be feeling like no one was considering me at all. And that I am supposed to forget about myself altogether, take over all of these roles, and like it too. I would be somewhat resentful, although I couldn't really admit it, because what a crummy way for a man to feel about a woman he loves at a difficult time in her life when I am supposed to be supportive."

What I had described to him were typical reactions to this situation. Although his feelings were typical and predictable, he didn't know that they were. As a child, he had only been allowed to express the feelings that his mother found acceptable. Gradually, over the years, he had learned to keep his feeings to himself. This was far more satisfactory than risking his mother's disapproval. In this circumstance, since he judged his feelings as inappropriate and didn't want to risk the disapproval of his wife, he kept them to himself.

He stared at me with his mouth open. He certainly felt as if I had taken off all of his clothes and that he was sitting there naked. Beth then said, "Of course you have all of those feelings, James. Of course you do. That's precisely the way I felt when you were in the hospital the last time and I had to take care of you."

You could feel the relief in that room. He found out that all of the feelings he had were O.K., that they were perfectly fine, natural, and NORMAL. He hadn't known that having all of those feelings didn't mean that he was a bastard and didn't care about his wife. He had to be told.

As soon as I had the information that he was an adult child of an alcoholic, it was not very difficult to focus on precisely what was giving this couple trouble.

As it happened, she recovered very quickly from the operation, he was able to be supportive, and the marriage is fine. She is more mindful of the fact that he simply does not know some things, and he understands that his reactions are not all that strange, especially the ones that he learned to suppress when he was a child.

2. **Children of alcoholics have difficulty in following a project through from beginning to end.**

The topic one evening in an adult children of alcoholics meeting was procrastination. When I asked them to talk about what it meant to them, the opening response was, "I'm the world's biggest procrastinator," or "Somehow I just don't seem to be able to finish anything that I start." When I asked some grown children of alcoholics to be a little bit more specific, this is what I heard:

Bob said, "I know what you mean. I'm facing that right now. I've been running into a problem at work trying to organize information and write it down on a piece of paper. I have this incredible difficulty seeing what it is and putting it down simply on a piece of paper. I sit and flounder until somebody says, 'What the hell are you doing? Do this and this and this, and I want this!' And all of a sudden it's obvious, and why the hell didn't I think about it? I'm scared. This is my job. It is essential to what I do now. I can't go on like this forever. I'm not going to be a six-month-newly-hired forever, and I'm alarmed."

Amy's statement went like this: "In organizing a long paper, I get stuck. I really wonder what the hell it is with me, I just can't plot it out. I've got all this stuff, and I can't sift it out. It's so hard for me not to abandon it, even if I'm interested in it, and I want to follow through with it. It's such a fucking struggle.

"When I was going to college, I had all these incompletes that turned to F's. The courses I did were all A's, but all the F's really sickened me. I'm scared, too, because it's affecting my job as well."

These comments are fairly typical, and it's not too hard to understand why a difficulty exists. These people are not procrastinators in the usual sense.

In the typical alcoholic home, there are an awful lot of promises.

The great job was always around the corner. The big deal was always about to be made. The work that needed to be done around the house would be done in no time. The toy that will be built—the go-cart, the doll house—and so on.

"I'm going to do this. I'm going to do that." But this or that never really happens. Not only doesn't it happen, the alcoholic wants credit even for having the idea, even for intending to do it. You grew up in this environment.

Remember the projects that got a little further than that? Painting the living room, for example. Remember when the alcoholic went out, bought the paint, came back, covered everything with the dropcloth, and it was years until the living room was finally painted? That is, unless your mother got disgusted somewhere along the way and painted it herself.

There were many projects like that. Lots of wonderful ideas, but never effected. If they were, so much time passed, you had forgotten about the original idea.

Who took the time to sit down with you when you had an idea for a project and said, "That's a good idea. How are you going to go about doing it? How long is it going to take you? What are the steps involved?'' Probably no one. When was it that one of your parents said, "Gee. That idea is terrific! You sure you can do it? Can you break it down into smaller pieces? Can you make it manageable?" Probably never.

This is not to suggest that ALL parents who do not live with alcohol teach their children how to solve problems. But it is to suggest that in a functional family, the child had this behavior and attitude to model. The child observes the process and the child may even ask questions along the way. The learning may be more indirect than direct, but it is present. Since your experience was so vastly different, it's no surprise to me that you have a problem following a project through from beginning to end. You haven't seen it happen, and you don't know how to make it happen. Lack of knowledge isn't the same as procrastination.

In the last section of this book, we are going to talk about how you can change this alarming state of affairs.

3.   **Adult children of alcoholics lie when it would be just as easy to tell the truth.**

Lying is basic to the family system affected by alcohol. It masquerades in part as overt denial of unpleasant realities, coverups, broken promises, and inconsistencies. It takes many forms and has many implications. Although it is somewhat different than the kind of lying usually talked about, it certainly is a departure from the truth.

The first and most basic lie is the family's denial of the problem. So the pretense that everything at home is in order is a lie, and the family rarely discusses the truth openly, even with each other. Perhaps somewhere in one's private thoughts there is a recognition of the truth, but there's also the struggle to deny it.

The next lie, the coverup, relates to the first one. The non-alcoholic family member covers up for the alcoholic member. As a child, you saw your non-alcoholic parent covering up for your alcoholic parent. You heard him or her on the phone, making excuses for your mother or father not fulfilling an obligation, not being on time. That's part of the lie that you lived.

You also heard a lot of promises from your alcoholic parent. These, too, turned out to be lies.

Lying as the norm in your house became part of what you knew and what could be useful to you. At times, it made life much more comfortable. If you lied about getting your work done, you could get away with being lazy for a while. If you lied about why you couldn't bring a friend home, or why you were late coming home, you could avert unpleasantness. It seemed to make life simpler for everybody.

Although your family said that telling the truth was a virtue, you knew they didn't mean much of what they said. So the truth lost its meaning.

Lying has become a habit. That's why the statement, "Adult children of alcoholics lie when it would be just as easy to tell the truth," is relevant. But if lying is what you have heard comes naturally, perhaps it is not as easy to tell the truth.

In this context, "It would be just as easy to tell the truth," means that you derive no real benefit from lying.

The following are comments made by adult children of alcoholics who are concerned about their lying. You will probably recognize yourself, at least in part.

Joan, a 26-year-old guidance counselor whose mother was alcoholic said, "I find myself lying, and about half way through the lie wanting to say, "Stop! That's a lie, that's not it. Let's start over again," but too embarrassed to do it. I don't know that I had to lie growing up. I just know that I did. I used to make up stories in order to be noticed, I think, and I think I feel bad that I didn't get caught, because if people had talked to me, and listened to me, and known me, they would have known that I was bullshitting, and I was really good at it. I'd start out faking being sick sometimes, and then get really sick. I was really an expert at it. It was so much easier to do that than to say that I just couldn't do what others could do. I felt like it would be terrible not to be able to cut it, I'd lose face. It was sad, though, and I didn't like doing it. There was always this panic about getting caught. I wouldn't have minded getting caught so I could stop the charade. It seemed to be because I didn't believe I could keep it up. I just didn't know how to do it, and then I would start making things up. It gets very complicated. There has been a need in the past to end friendships because I couldn't keep track of the lies anymore. I want to stop lying. I really want to stop it. When I find myself in the middle of one, I'm just scared to death. I just want to say, 'Hold it,' and back up, and go to the truth. I really don't know what to do. When it's just an inconsequential, silly little dumb thing, I feel like an asshole."

Jeff, a 30-year-old engineer with two recovering alcoholic parents said, "I can remember an occasion when I told a really big lie. I was on a hiking trip in the White Mountains with some friends of mine. We were hiking from one hut to another place a few miles away in the snow. The temperature dropped and it was really, really cold. I had skipped breakfast, we were in a real hurry to get packed, and I had just eaten some candy bars or something. I ran after the rest of them. On the way over, we started to get strung out. The wind was blowing very hard, and there was snow all over the place. I began to fall behind the others, and I remember being in extreme resentment that they wouldn't slow up and wait for me, but at the same time I was annoyed at myself that I couldn't keep up with them. I had gotten this book on hypothermia. I knew how to do it, and I faked them. I slowed up behind them, and part of the symptoms were to get vague and hazy mentally, so I started to wander off the trail. By the time they got together and started wondering where I was, we had wasted a good hour. They came back and did all of the things that go along with trying to pull someone out of hypothermia. I really wanted that attention, and I guess I had just reached the point where I was willing to do just about anything to get it. They were leaving me. I was slipping behind and nobody had noticed. We were in the mountains and I could freeze to death, and with the statements I made to myself, it was easy to make the progression. All right, I am, I'm gonna freeze to death. We'll see how you respond when I come down with hypothermia.

"In reality, I had spent 200 dollars on the fancy equipment, and I could have laid in the snow for a month without freezing to death. So, I simply faked it. I was nervous about getting caught. I knew how to do it, but I wasn't physically able to do what the other guys were doing.

"I knew that when I was growing up the truth was irrelevant. When my parents were three sheets to the wind, it didn't matter what you said or what you didn't say. When my mother was drunk, she was in her own world, and the conversation revolved around the age of the washing machine or the refrigerator, or something like that. I just didn't come into it. There was no 'Your grades aren't good enough' or anything like that. I just wasn't there.

"The same thing is pretty much true of my father. He was isolated also. So, there wasn't any truth or lying. You could say anything you liked. You could dance naked with a rose in your teeth, they simply wouldn't notice."

Steve, a 36-year-old alcoholism counselor with two alcoholic parents said, "What about wanting to survive? When I was a kid, I became a very accomplished liar, mostly by selecting what I would say. Whenever my father asked me something, if I gave him a straight answer he would always criticize the answer. I stopped giving him a straight answer, and I realized that it worked very well. If he criticized the not-straight answer, I could discard the criticism as being of no practical value, because what I gave him wasn't true anyway. Over the years, I've kept that. Ninety-eight percent of the time I'm honest, and I have a reputation for honesty, but I always keep that other 2% in reserve. I think I started keeping my lies down to a minimum with other people, because I got into a thing of not being able to remember what it was that I said.

"I have to distinguish between lying about things and lying about feelings. When it comes to feelings, I have a tough time being honest about my feelings, being honest with myself and honest with others.

"In my family, my mother had a reputation for being a pathological liar, and I suspected that in order to get any attention at all, I had to make things bigger than they really were. I mean, especially to get recognition from my parents. When my parents were drunk, one or both of them, it was easy to lie and get away with it. They weren't dealing with things very well either. If I came up with a story sometimes, I really got the feeling that they preferred that to the truth. They didn't want to know, as long as I wasn't arrested or causing them any embarrassment.

"I soon learned that telling the truth was probably the worst possible thing I could do. Lying was O.K., and I just needed to be smart enough to cover up. I rarely ever got into trouble, so my credibility was rarely questioned."

Sandra, a 23-year-old child of two alcoholic parents said, "Lying is one thing I absolutely will not tolerate in other people. My ex-husband lied to me before we were married and it almost broke us up. I lie to myself constantly and don't know it. I'll fabricate an idea or concept and I'll say that's what I feel and I'll believe it with every inch of me. Somewhere down the road, just like a smack in the face, I'll say to myself, 'You don't believe that.' I've been deluding myself the whole time, and I still can do that—lie to myself—but I do have a lot of trouble lying to other people. That is to say, I won't deliberately lie. But, if it gets to the point where I have to be too honest, then I've been known to end the friendship. I will walk away when it becomes work to be honest.

"There are very few people with whom I'm honest about my feelings. I can feel absolutely shattered inside and someone will ask me how I'm doing, and I'll say, 'Fine.'

"In my job I'm honest, but I don't share, so what's there to be dishonest about? In A.A., I share somewhat. I don't share all that much. The times I'm really honest, people look at me like I'm strange.

"I think of myself as being honest because I was the minister's daughter, and thou shalt not lie. And now, thinking about this, I realized that my mother never believed me. She never believed me when I was a kid growing up.

"One time I ran home from school and some kids had been throwing rocks at me. I got home and told my mom and she said, 'That didn't happen. You're lying.' I was out of breath, I was exhausted, there were tears rolling down my face, and she didn't believe me. It happened all the time.

"One time some kids dragged me down some brick steps and scraped my back up. She didn't believe it happened. She didn't believe kids would do that to her daughter. I felt as though I was hitting my head against a brick wall and nothing was getting through.

"That's probably why I'm so careful what I share today. I don't want to not be believed, if I'm telling the truth. I don't want to take that risk. So, I would prefer to share very little."

These people, in discussing what lying means to them in their lives, have a high level of self-awareness and a fearless honesty with which they share their difficulty in telling the truth. It is the first step of changing this aspect of their personalities. If you wish, you can change too.

4. Adult children of alcoholics judge themselves without mercy.

When you were a child, there was no way that you were good enough. You were constantly criticized. You believed that your family would be better off without you, because you were the cause of the trouble. You may have been criticized for things that made no sense. "If you weren't such a rotten kid, I wouldn't have to drink." It makes no sense, but if you hear something often enough, for a long-enough period of time, you will end up believing it. As a result, you internalized these criticisms as negative self-feelings . They remain, even though no one is saying them to you any more.

Since there is no way for you to meet the standards of perfection that you have internalized from childhood, you are always falling short of the mark you have set for yourself. As a child, whatever you did was not quite good enough. No matter how hard you tried, you should have tried harder. If you got an A, it should have been an A+. You were never good enough. I have a client who told me that his mother was so demanding that when he was in basic training, he found the sergeants loose. So, this became a part of you, who you are, a part of the way you see yourself. The shoulds and should nots can become paralyzing after a while.

One aspect of this is how some people are able to successfully maintain a negative self-image when there is evidence to the contrary. This is how it works. If anything goes wrong, it is your responsibility. Somehow, you should have done it differently and things would have been better. Anything that goes right has to do with something other than yourself. It was going to happen that way anyway. Or, if it is very clear that you are the one who is responsible for a positive outcome, you dismissed it with, "Oh that was easy. That was of little consequence."

This is really not a sense of humility, but a distortion of reality. It feels safer to keep a negative self-image, because you are used to it. Accepting praise for being competent means changing the way you see yourself, and means that maybe you can judge yourself a little less harshly—and be a little more accepting and say, "I made that mistake, however, I am not a mistake."

An example of the kind of automatic judgment that I hear is very well exemplified in Ellen's statement. She talks about having an operation and coming home from the hospital. She calls her mother, who comes to take care of her.

"O.K. I'm the one who has had the surgery, and my mother starts attacking each of my friends as they walk in the door to see me. She had a royal fight with one of my friends, just tore her head off, and my friend just tore her head off. By the end of the night, I was taking care of my mother. I was the one who was getting my mother some hot tea to calm her nerves, when what I needed was some tea, and some loving, and some sympathy. But, I really know that the only reason I got mad at my mother was because she was not taking care of me *my* way. She wasn't doing it the way I wanted her to do it, and I was being very selfish."

Ellen found herself to be at fault, because she wanted things done her way. She judged herself for not feeling well and for wanting to be taken care of.

She said to me, "I always do that. That is one of the strongest parts of who I am. It's that I judge everything I do, and it's partly because everything is so black and white. It's either all bad or all good. There's no middle ground. Most of what I see myself doing is bad, even though intellectually I feel that it's good, emotionally I can't."

What Ellen said is fairly typical. I was working with another client of mine on "shoulds." She had reached the point where she was completely immobilized and I asked her to make a list of all the "shoulds" she gave herself in a day. The list was enormous. When she was able to look at it objectively, she laughed and said, "I'm going to stop judging myself. I'm not going to judge myself, even if I'm entirely at fault."

Judging yourself negatively is one of the things that you do best, because it is ingrained in your personality. Sometimes there's even a sort of pleasure or a comfort in it.

The adult children of alcoholics I know who have joined A.A. and Al-Anon absolutely cannot wait to get to the fourth and fifth steps. The fourth step is, "Took a searching and fearless moral inventory of ourselves." And the fifth step is, "Admitted to God, to ourselves, and to another human being the exact nature of our wrongs."

When I see them doing these steps shortly after joining the program, I know what they will do. They see Steps Four and Five as a good opportunity to come down on themselves. They judge themselves on characteristics that they never even knew they had. All of these characteristics are negative. There's never a positive characteristic in it. It has never been used positively. They take to it like a duck to water. Then, the idea that they can flagellate themselves to somebody else is absolutely super.

If I suggest that maybe counseling is a form of moral inventory, that maybe it could be done formally a little later, it makes no difference. There is no way to slow them down. I issue a warning that they're going to do a giant number on themselves. They do it anyway, then come back and I get to help pick up the pieces. We move on. At a little later stage, they do the fourth and fifth steps much more successfully. But initially, it's a great opportunity to come down on themselves.

Your judgment of others is not nearly as harsh as your judgment of yourself, although it is hard for you to see other people's behavior in terms of a continuum either. Black and white, good or bad, are typically the way you look at things. Either side is an awesome responsibility. You know what it feels like to be bad, and how those feelings make you behave. And then, if you are good, there is always the risk that it won't last. So, either way, you set yourself up. Either way there is a great amount of pressure on you at all times. How difficult and stressful life is. How hard it is to just sit back and relax and say, "It's O.K. to be me."

5.   **Adult children of alcoholics have difficulty having fun.**
6.   **Adult children of alcoholics take themselves very seriously.**

These two characteristics are very closely linked. If you're having trouble having fun, you're probably taking yourself very seriously, and if you don't take yourself all that seriously, chances are you can have fun.

Once again, in order to understand this problem, you need to look back at your chldhood. How much fun was your childhood?

You don't have to answer that. Children of alcoholics simply don't have much fun. One child of an alcoholic described it as "chronic trauma." You didn't hear your parents laughing and joking and fooling around. Life was a very serious, angry business. You didn't really learn to play with the other kids. You could join in some of the games, but were you really able to let yourself go and have fun? Even if you could have, it was discouraged. The tone around the house put a damper on your fun. Eventually, you just went along with everybody else. Having fun just wasn't fun. There was no place for it in your house. You gave it up. It just wasn't a workable idea. The spontaneous child within was squashed.

Last summer, at a camp for children of alcoholic parents, the staff, who were mostly adult children of alcoholics, were playing for probably the first time in their lives. "The only other camp I ever went to was in Vietnam," said one of the counselors. Others reported that it was the very first time they had thrown a frisbee. They were becoming very childlike in that they were having fun and it was a new experience.

So it's really no wonder that you don't have fun. You may even disapprove of others who act silly, thinking, "Oh look, she's making such a fool of herself." But in a little place inside of you, you really wish you could do that, too.

At the Rutgers Summer School for Alcohol Studies, some of us were throwing a ball around, and others were watching. Some adult children of alcoholics told me later how badly they wanted to join in. "I wanted to get up and join in so badly, but I just couldn't get up and do it. I didn't want to make a fool of myself. I didn't want to look foolish."

The spontaneous child that got squashed so many years ago struggles to be released. The pressure to be adult helps to keep the child repressed. You are at war with yourself. But fear of the unknown wins out. After all, what would happen if that child gained freedom. What would it mean. So you rationalize.

Having fun, being silly, being childlike, is being foolish. It is no wonder that adult children of alcoholics have difficulty having fun. Life is too serious.

You also have trouble separating yourself from your work, so you take yourself very seriously at whatever job you have to do. You can take the work seriously, but not yourself. You are therefore a prime candidate for burnout.

One night on the subject of work, Abby turned to me with a very angry face and said, "You may make me laugh at myself, but I want you to know, I don't think it's funny."

7. Adult children of alcoholics have difficulty with intimate relationships.

Adult children want very much to have healthy, intimate relationships, and it is extraordinarily difficult for a number of reasons.

The first, and most obvious reason is that they have no frame of reference for a healthy, intimate relationship, because they have never seen one. The only model they have is their parents, which you and I both know was not healthy.

They also carry with them the experience of come close, go away—the inconsistency of a loving parent-child relationship. They feel loved one day and rejected the next. The fear of being abandoned is a terrible fear they grow up with. If the fear isn't overwhelming, it certainly gets in the way. Not knowing what it is like to have a consistent, day-to-day, healthy, intimate relationship with another person makes building one very painful and complicated.

The push-pull, approach-avoidance, the "I want you—go away," the colossal terror of being close, yet the desire and need for it is beautifully shown in a poem by John Gould.

WHY DO YOU COME?

I don't want you.
I don't need you.
I don't want to see you.
Yet you keep coming back.
I can't figure you out.
A pretty girl like you
Should be able to find
Someone else.
I reject you and
Yet you keep
Returning.
Everywhere I turn,
You're there.
You're just taking
Up too much of

My time.
Why do you come?
Why don't you leave?
You are?
Good!
What did you want
With a guy like me?
Love.
Please come back.
She's gone.

John Gould

The following demonstrates the same conflict. Sam was involved in one of his first relationships and describes what happened.

"Last week Cindy brought me some fruit. I drink a lot of Hawaiian Punch. She had cut some labels from the cans, put them on the fruit, and brought them and gave them to me. I felt like crying. She thought my nutrition wasn't good enough or something, and she was going to bring me this fruit. She didn't just bring me the fruit. She went and stuck those stupid little labels on them!"

It meant so much to him that he wanted to cry, but he had to find a way to diminish it. Push, pull. The internal struggle goes on and on.

Karen talks about it from another vantage point. She has the same confusion as an adult because of her past experiences.

"It's so much easier to deal with deep negative emotions about myself, especially in terms of my relationships with men. I'm rejecting of anybody who's willing to love me. I have this feeling that the only way I'm ever going to fall in love with somebody is if they are absolutely perfect and they walk in the door and it's an automatic, instantaneous, perfect relationship. Otherwise, I don't want any part of it. I'll get interested in somebody, start going after them, and the second they're interested in me, I don't want any part of it at all. It's just completely gone. It's gotten to the point where most of the time I don't bother, because I know what I'm going to do anyway, so why even bother trying? I'm not sure if I'm afraid of loving, or if I'm afraid of being loved. The only thing that comes to mind is that I'm afraid of not ever knowing that love is real, or if the love is real, having it taken away, somehow."

Thus, the fear of abandonment gets in the way of the developing of a relationship. The development of any healthy relationship requires a lot of give and take, and problem solving. There is always some disagreement and anger which a couple resolve. A minor disagreement gets very big, very quickly for adult children of alcoholics, because the issue of being abandoned takes precedence over the original issue.

Karen is deeply affected by concern over abandonment.

"I take everything so seriously with relationships. If I don't feel like I'm being treated in the right way, I react with anger and panic, and 'Oh, my God!' I'll get really uptight and I'll say something and react with anger, but I know that they're not going to want to stay with me. Somehow I'm not worth it. I always see them as being all right. It's always that even if I feel I'm worth it, they leave anyway and there's nothing I can do to make them stay, and it's easy to make them leave somehow. I feel as though I'm always having to do things to make them stay. And it's not me doing things because it's me and I'm doing them. I'm doing things to make them stay or keep them from leaving. It's always like 'Don't leave me.' "

These same feelings are expressed by Nancy.

"I have a real strong panic reaction to someone's anger with me. The panic that I experience is so extreme that I really don't know what to do with it, so that whenever there's a small argument, the fear is so great that it always escalates, and I guess I would love to know how people handle rejection, because to me it becomes more of an issue of abandonment."

As a result of the fear of abandonment, you don't feel confident about yourself. You don't feel good about yourself, or believe that you are lovable. So you look to others for what it is that you cannot give yourself in order to feel O.K. You feel O.K. if someone else tells you that you are O.K. Needless to say, you give away a great deal of power. In a relationship, you give the other person the power to lift you up or knock you down. You feel wonderful if they treat you well and tell you that you are wonderful, but when they don't, these feelings no longer belong to you.

Some clear examples of this came through in one of the groups of children of alcoholics that I ran:

Ed said, "I fear rejection. I'm very dependent. All the time that I'm involved with the group, I'm looking for praises from Jan. I know that that's dumb. It would be nice, but I would like to not have that need. I would like to wean myself off that need to constantly seek approval for everything that I do. It's a pain in the ass and it occupies a lot of my time. I'm constantly fighting for the audience."

Ray agreed with him. "I've wondered about that in myself, too. I wonder about struggling in front of audiences who approve of people who are trying to come together to work on themselves, because I am sure that that generates approval. The thought has occured to me that maybe sometimes what I'm doing in becoming a part of the group is just a very sophisticated mechanism for getting approval."

These overwhelming fears of being abandoned or rejected prevent any ease in the process of developing a relationship. Coupled with a sense of urgency, "This is the only time I have; if I don't do it now, it will never happen," tend to put pressure on the relationship. It makes it much more difficult to evolve slowly, to let two people get to know each other better, and to explore each other's feelings and attitudes in a variety of ways.

This sense of urgency makes the other person feel smothered, even though it is not the intent. I know a couple who have tremendous problems because whenever they argue, she panics and worries that he is now going to leave her. She needs constant reassurance in the middle of the argument that he's not going to leave her, and that he still loves her. When he is in conflict, which is difficult for him as well, he tends to want to withdraw and be by himself. Needless to say, this makes the issue at hand more difficult to resolve than if it were only the issue itself needing to be confronted.

The feelings of being insecure, of having difficulty in trusting, and questions about whether or not you're going to get hurt, are not exclusive to adult children of alcoholics. These are problems most people have. Few people enter a relationship fully confident that things are going to work out the way they hope they will. They enter a relationship hopeful, but with a variety of fears.

So, all of the things that cause you concern are not unique to you. It's simply a matter of degree: your being the child of an alcoholic caused the ordinary difficulties to become more severe.

Adult children of alcoholics do not appear to have any more or any fewer sexual problems than the general population.

In talking with many adult children of alcoholics about their sexuality, I found that their conversations, their attitudes, and their feelings were no different from any other group. The hangups that some of them had related more to the church and the culture than what went on at home. This is not to say that some pretty bizarre things did not go on at home. This is to say that what went on in the alcoholic home was no more or less bizarre than things I've heard of or seen going on in other kinds of homes.

Professionals in the alcohol field are now taking a look at the problem of incest. We are trying very hard to understand it in order to help to effect healthy changes in our clients. I doubt that alcoholics are any more guilty of incest than anybody else. It may be that incest occurs more often when the adult is drunk than when the adult is sober, but we're talking about alcoholics here, not about someone who is disinhibited from alcohol.

With respect to sex in general, the children of alcoholics have not been able to sit down with their parents and discuss it. However, I don't believe this is exclusive to them. Talking about sexuality is difficult for people, regardless of whether or not they are living with alcoholism. Somehow, it's easier to excuse within the alcoholic family system. If you're in too much of a squirrel cage to discuss anything, sex is just like anything else.

We know that the sexual relationship of the parents breaks down as does every other form of communication. We know that offering and withdrawing of sex becomes a weapon, and we know that the experience becomes unhealthy between the two partners, as other things become unhealthy. I know that sex is used as a weapon in households that are not affected by alcoholism.

I am not suggesting that the adult child of the alcoholic is necessarily healthy in terms of sexual attitudes. I am just not suggesting that they are not. It has been my experience that adult children of alcoholics have no more, or no fewer, problems with their sexuality than anybody else.

8. **Adult children of alcoholics over-react to changes over which they have no control.**

This is very simple to understand. The young child of the alcoholic was not in control. The alcoholic's life was inflicted on him, as was his environment.

In order to survive when growing up, he needed to turn that around. He needed to begin taking charge of his environment. This became very important, and remains so. The child of the alcoholic learns to trust himself more than anyone else when it's impossible to rely on somebody's else's judgment.

As a result, you are very often accused of being controlling, rigid, and lacking in spontanaeity. This is probably true. It doesn't come from wanting to do everything your own way. It isn't because you are spoiled or unwilling to listen to other ideas. It comes from the fear that if you are not in charge, if a change is made, abruptly, quickly, without your being able to participate in it, you will lose control of your life.

There is no question that this is overreaction. And when there is an overreaction, it generally means that it is caused by something in one's past experience. At the moment, the thing you overreacted to may seem foolish to others. But it is an automatic response. "You can't do that to me. No, I will not go to the movies when we decided we were going roller skating." It's almost an involuntary reflex.

When you look back on your reactions and your behavior later, you feel somewhat foolish, but at the time you were simply unable to shift gears.

9. **Adult children of alcoholics constantly seek approval and affirmation.**

> *Searching eyes,*
> *Questioning all corners of the room*
> *in split seconds—*
> *Brows which aspire*
> *to the heights of the forehead;*
> *darting, cool and somewhat unsure fingers*
> *examining the air around her—*
> *reassuring her doubtful mind*
> *of the truth of her existence;*
> *Seeing herself in the mirrors of others' minds,*

She rarely believes her own—
accepting her existence as a reflection
the haze rarely clears,
the mirror is a glass
and her soul is bare
Does she know that she is her own—
For real.

Marya DePinto

We talk about an external and an internal locus of control. When a child is born, the environment pretty much dictates how he is going to feel about himself. The school, the church and other people all have an influence, but the most important influence is what we call "significant others." In the child's world, this means his parents. So the child begins to believe who he is by the messages that he gets from his parents. And as he gets older, these messages become internalized and contribute significantly to his self image. The movement is toward the internal locus of control.

The message you got as a child was very confused. It was not unconditional love. It was not, "I think *you're* terrific; but, I'm not too happy about what you just did." The definitions were not clear, and the messages were mixed. "Yes, no, I love you, go away." So you grew up with some confusion about yourself. The affirmations you didn't get on a day-to-day basis as a child, you interpret as negative.

Now, when affirmation is offered, it's very difficult to accept. Accepting the affirmation would be the beginning of changing your self-image.

Lou had this very problem, but was beginning to change.
"In the last four months at work, a lot of people have come up to me and said, 'You're a really nice person. I'm glad you're here.' People have said this more than once, and I have a tough time accepting that. I wonder what's going to come after that. 'Lou, you're a nice person, but ...' That's what I heard in my childhood. 'But' was always devastating. What I'm doing with that now is I'm saying, 'Thank you.' I'm still wondering about the but, but I'm beginning to believe that I'm the one that's putting it there and they're not."

Another member in the group talked about a relationship he backed away from because the affirmation would cause him to change. He said, "After last week, it occurred to me that perhaps the reason why the relationship didn't get anywhere is because Cindy did like me, and since she did like me—I judged her as being worthless."

Anyone who could care about him could not be worth very much. This self-defeating reasoning resulting in his losing the affirmation and approval that he wanted so desperately.

10.   Adult children of alcoholics feel that they are different from other people.

Children of alcoholics feel different from other people because to some degree they actually are. Yet, there are more of them than they are aware of.

They also assume that in any group of people, everyone else feels comfortable and they are the only ones who feel awkward. This is not peculiar to them. Never, of course, does anyone check it out and find out that each person has his own way of trying not to look awkward. Is that true of you, too?

Interestingly enough, you even feel different in a group of adult children of alcoholics. Feeling different is something you have had with you since childhood, and even if the circumstance does not warrant it, the feeling prevails. Other children had an opportunity to be children. You didn't. You were very much concerned with what was going on at home. You could never be completely comfortable playing with other children. You could not be fully there. Your concerns about your home problems clouded everything else in your life.

What happened to you is what happened to the rest of your family. You became isolated. As a result, socializing, being a part of any group, became increasingly difficult. You simply did not develop the social skills necessary to feel comfortable or a part of the group.

You guessed at what would work. Dana tried bribes. "I used to have this thing about Barbie Dolls. I had such an incredible collection of them, and I used to give my prized ones away to people so I would have a friend. Usually they thought I was a jerkoff for giving it away and thought less of me."

Dave said, "I lent my books. My books were my most prized possessions."

Another child of an alcoholic said, "I tend to give people what ever they need at that moment, so that's a hook into them to like me and maybe I try to get the hook in first. As a child, I watched how my father manipulated people this way, and I saw how well it worked for him, so I guess I thought it would work for me the same way."

On the subject of picking a role model, Dana reports: "I kind of pick people with this unrealistic image in terms of being the bright ones, the smart ones, the loving ones, the Peace Corps types. I'd pick role models that were just sweet, kind, loving, and that kind of stuff. I don't pick people who are appropriate, but who seem perfect. I never picked anyone who was a bully or a tyrant to model myself after. I would look at that and think that that is not the way it should be, but I do know that the people I picked were not appropriate."

Dave agreed. "When I was a kid, I used to pick inappropriate role models also. But I went to the other extreme. All the people I hung out with were worse than I was. I picked out all the teenage alcoholics, the guys that drank codeine cough syrup, women who could not have close sexual relationships with men. I was very frustrated as an adolescent. I picked out the fat ones. I would not dare to date a good-looking woman. I still have very few friends."

It is hard for children of alcoholics to believe that they can be accepted because of who they are, and that the acceptance does not have to be earned.

Feeling different and somewhat isolated is part of your makeup.

11. Adult children of alcoholics are either super responsible or super irresponsible.

You take it all on or your give it all up. There is no middle ground. You tried to please your parents, doing more and more and more, or you reached the point where you recognized it didn't matter, so you did nothing. You also did not see a family that cooperated with each other. You didn't have a family that decided on Sunday, "Let's all work in the yard. I will work on this and you work on that, and then we'll come together."

Not having a sense of doing a part of a project, of how to cooperate with other people and let all the parts come together and become a whole, you either do all of it or you do none of it. You also don't have a good sense of your own limitations. Saying no is extraordinarily difficult for you so you do more and more and more. You do it, not because you really have a bloated sense of yourself, but rather (1) because you don't have a realistic sense of your capacity; or (2) because if you say 'no,' you are afraid that they will find you out. They will find out that you are incompetent. The quality of the job you do does not seem to influence your feelings about yourself. So you take on more and more and more and more. Until you finally burn out.

The constant fear of being found out takes much of your energy. It even takes some of the energy that you could be using to do a better job. Not better in terms of what the employer asks for, because you're probably giving the employer more than he ask for, but better in being more efficient.

Dana talked about her feelings about herself on the job.

"Nobody has said anything. Nobody has complained about my work. If anything, they've praised it. They've all been good to me. They've been very understanding when I've been sick, and I am still there looking for the pink slip. And the thing is, I know I'm doing a good job. It's just that I'm so insecure, and that insecurity overrides any good thing that I'm doing. I continue to wait to be fired."

Because of her insecurity, this is the way she behaves.

"I've been getting myself crazy in terms of organization, scheduling my time and energy in such a small place, that the pressure I put on myself is incredible. It sent me to my office in such a state today that when one more piece of 'I want you' was handed me, I started to cry. I seem to have this responsibility thing where I feel I have to take it all on, whether it's responsible for me to do it or not. I want to be able to do it, and I think I should be able to do it."

She finally worked herself up to this point.

"I'm not going in to work tomorrow. There's no way in hell that I'm going in to work tomorrow. I don't think I have any time left and I know that I'm going to be docked, but I just can't go in there anymore. Not this week. I can't go in and look at those people and work. I can't work. I can't do anything. I'm just blocked. It's frustrating as hell. I had a lot of work today, and I was sick to my stomach. I got home and I was hysterical. Walking around, pacing around, and I tried calling everybody and nobody was home. The whole world's out to lunch. I'm sorry. It's gotten to the point where I don't think I can manage anything."

In talking to a group of adult children of alcoholics, I said somewhat sarcastically, "You book your days so full that there is no time even to go to the bathroom." One young man responded to me by saying, "That's not true. We do plan time to go to the bathroom. It's just that we bring a book along."

12. Adult children of alcoholics are extremely loyal, even in the face of evidence that the loyalty is undeserved.

The alcoholic home appears to be a very loyal place. Family members hang in long after reasons dictate that they should leave. The so-called "loyalty" is more the result of fear and insecurity than anything else; nevertheless, the behavior that is modeled is one where no one walks away just because the going gets rough. This sense enables the adult child to remain in involvements that are better dissolved.

Since making a friend or developing a relationship is so difficult and so complicated, once the effort has been made it is permanent. If someone cares enough about you to be your friend, your lover, or your spouse, then you have the obligation to stay with them forever. If you have let them know who you are, if they have discovered who you are and not rejected you, that fact, in and of itself, is enough to make you sustain the relationship. The fact that they may treat you poorly does not matter. You can rationalize that. Somehow, no matter what they do, or say, you can figure out a way to excuse their behavior and find yourself at fault. This reinforces your negative self-image and enables you to stay in the relationship. Your loyalty is unparalleled.

There is also a lot of safety in an established relationship. It is known, and the known is always more secure than the unknown. Change being extremely difficult, you would much prefer to stay with what is.

You also don't know much about what a good relationship is all about. So you stay with what you have, not knowing that there could be anything better or anything different. You just muddle your way through.

On this subject, Dana said:

"It was like once I made a commitment, I was going to stick to it. It was because I was so scared of being myself. I didn't know that there were other types of marriages other than the type my parents had, or the type that his parents had. I wanted my marriage to work so that we would be able to buy a house, have babies, and do all the things right, and be happy and contented, and like each other, and love each other. It didn't work out that way, but I couldn't let go."

13. **Adult children of alcoholics are impulsive. They tend to lock themselves into a course of action without giving serious consideration to alternative behaviors or possible consequences. This impulsivity leads to confusion, self-loathing, and loss of control over their environment. In addition, they spend an excessive amount of energy cleaning up the mess.**

This can best be characterized as "alcoholic." It may be modeled behavior without any conscious awareness. For example: The alcoholic gets an idea. "I'm going to stop off and have a (one) drink on the way home." Simple idea—any thoughts that would get in the way of carrying out this idea are rationalized away. "I promised to be home on time." — "One drink will not make me late," or, "I promised I'd stop drinking" — "one drink is not drinking."

It is true that one drink will not make him late nor is it "drinking" within his framework, if he simply has one drink. So he stops for "the" drink.

From the time that the idea entered the alcoholic's head to have the drink, he was compelled. No other options were available. The idea extended only to the first drink.

The rest of the scenario is clear. After the first drink, the compulsion takes over, and the alcoholic has lost control. He rationalizes for a while, and then is so far into it that he loses sight of what he had in his mind to begin with.

The idea that triggers the impulsive behavior has no time frame. It is the "here and now." No serious consideration is paid to what happened the last time, nor what the consequences will be this time.

Since the idea is limited to the moment, "I'm going to have a (one) drink," thoughts of "I'll get drunk and be late and this will cause trouble," simply are not relevant. That fact that there will be loss of control and that the behavior will get out of hand is simply ignored. "I can control what I drink," is heard over and over and evidence to the contrary is similarly dismissed, once the compulsion takes over and the uncontrolled behavior begins.

Impulsivity is a very childlike quality. Ordinarily, children are impulsive. But when you were a child you were more of a parent than a child, so your present impulsive behavior is something you missed during your childhood. If you miss out on one stage, quite often you make it up at another time in your life. When a child has a parent who functions as a parent, and the child acts out impulsively, they say, "You cannot do that. Because you did that, there is a consequence."

As a child, you could not predict the outcome of any given behavior, so you don't know how to do it now. Also, there was no consistency at home. As a result, you haven't the following framework of "When I behaved impulsively in the past, this happened and that happened, and this person reacted in that way." Sometimes it would go O.K., and sometimes it wouldn't. Essentially, it may not have really mattered. Nor did anyone say to you, "These are the possible consequences of that behavior. Let's talk about other things that you might do."

The situation is further complicated by a terrible sense of urgency. If you don't do it immediately, you will not get a second chance. And you are used to being on the edge of a precipice, living from crisis to crisis. If things go smoothly, it's even more unsettling than when you're in a crisis. So it's not surprising that you may even create a crisis.

This impulsive behavior is not deliberate or calculated. It is behavior over which you have lost control. This is the characteristic that is most unsettling to you, that frightens the most, and that you really want to change.

Rose expresses it this way:

"It's not that I don't emphathize with other people, because when I see the effect my behavior has, when it happens I can't believe I've done that. I care about that person, how could I have? I'm absolutely flipped out that it's me. I do care about the impact, but somewhere between the impact and doing something about it, I have some kind of tunnel vision."

Dana: "I don't ever set out to intentionally hurt somebody else or to upset anybody else; it's just that that's the path I take and I just plunge right into it."

Mike: "It's like a plow. I mean, it's not something you do casually. I go full steam ahead."

Dana: "I'm walking forward with a wall on either side, and I just go."

Cindy: "My capacity to think, to hear words in my head, disappears. I'm not aware of finding any words to fit together in a sentence. It just becomes a mass of energy. I seem to bolt out."

Mike: "It gives me bad judgment and that bothers me."

Cindy: "I only see in the moment."

Dana: "Sometimes it's like that's the only path I can take. It's not really a path, but it's the only action. There have been times when I knew this was the wrong thing to do and I've paid the consequences four or five months down the road. I knew before I even went into it that it was the wrong thing to do."

Cindy: "Once the feelings take over, I have to go with it. It has a propulsion that I'm powerless against. I wish a crane would come down and pick me up out of it."

Dana: "Once I take the first step, that's all that's needed. It's like going down a hill. You take that first step, and it's all of a sudden rolling."

Cindy: "It seems like a commitment to go with whatever decision I make."

Sam: "It's very rigid with me. It's not that I start out to hurt somebody, but that the other person usually gets hurt in the process. Almost always somebody gets hurt. Even after I recognize it, I keep on going anyway. Whatever my agenda is, I adhere to it rigidly. There's a great deal of momentum behind it. There's a lot of energy and it just keeps right on barreling through. There's this concept of blinders. I may have been told facts that would slow another person down, or to check something out, but once I'm on this thing, rarely do I check things out. And if I do, I rarely listen."

Cindy: "It becomes compulsive, and I seem to lose the ability to project myself into the future to see what it really would be like, to see if that's really what I want to do. In the moment, if I'm feeling something negative with somebody, I seem to have a complete inability to feel and touch and taste the parts that are good, even though I know they are there. I can't feel them, so they are of no worth to me somehow."

Dana: "The emotion that I feel in the present is usually the only one that counts. I only feel the emotion I'm in at the time. It's so hard for me to remember that I can feel anything else but what I'm feeling at the moment. Or, that tomorrow

I'll look at this and feel differently."

As a result of this behavior, more often than not, the light at the end of the tunnel is the headlamp of an oncoming train. You have not been able to see the reaction or the implications of what you do. As a result, you create many outrageous situations for yourself.

A client decided one afternoon to buy a horse. She brought the horse home and put it in the garage. It was very difficult for her to understand why her husband was very upset, because it seemed like a good idea at the time. Once she had the idea, that was the end of it. She had to follow through. She could not stop herself.

You find that you will quit a job without realizing that you have no other means of support. You'll marry without really getting to know the other person. Buying horses is very unusual. I have only encountered that once, but the second two happen very, very often. You end up very concerned about your behavior, but before you can begin to look at it and change it, you have to spend a great deal of time and energy extricating yourself from a mess. So it is self-defeating on several levels.

Part of the difficulty is that adult children of alcoholics tend to look for immediate, as opposed to deferred, gratification.

The word I use most with my clients who are adult children of alcoholics is "patience." Whatever it is that comes up, whatever it is that you need to accomplish—be it emotionally, or behaviorally— you want to accomplish it yesterday. You have some difficulty in being patient with others. The person that you are most impatient with, however, is yourself. You want it all immediately.

This gets you into a lot of trouble, because your lack of patience feeds into everything else that gives you difficulty. Especially, it feeds into your impulsivity, your judgment of yourself.

It's not very hard to understand why it is that you want everything immediately. Putting things off gives you so much trouble because when you were growing up, if you did not get what you asked for in that very moment, that was the end of it. If you said, "I want this now," and your parents said, "You can't do it now, but you can do it by the end of the week," or, "We can talk about it later," you knew that was the end of it. You knew that promises for the future were broken. That was one consistent thing in your life.

That was the reality of your life. If you didn't do it immediately, it simply would not happen. This makes it very difficult for you to plan for the future. For you to say, "This is what I'm going to do two years from now, and this is the manner in which I am going to do it," is very much of a struggle. You want what you want when you want it, because a little part of you knows, even though it is probably no longer true, that if you don't get it now, if you didn't go after it now, if you don't grab on now, and grab on tight, it will never happen.

The sense of, "This is my last chance," is with you all the time. You even become impatient with yourself when you decide to work on patience, and don't become patient immediately. Patience, therefore, is something that you must work very hard to acquire.

3

breaking the cycle

1.   Adult children of alcoholics guess at what normal is.

It is important for you to recognize that there is no such thing as normal. This is the foundation of the issues that will be discussed. It is critical, because something built on a false premise can develop logically, but won't work. Like a house of cards, if the base is not secure, a small breeze will blow down the whole structure.

Normal is a myth like Santa Claus and the Brady Bunch. It is not realistic to talk in terms of normal, since it is something you have been fooled into believing exists. Other concepts like functional or dysfunctional are more useful. What is functional for you? What works well for you? What is in your best interest? And, in the best interest of your family? This approach is realistic and varies from person to person, from family to family.

The task, then, is not to find out what normal is, but to discover what is most comfortable for you and for those who are close to you. You bought the myth of normalcy, and in so doing, developed fantasies about your ideal self, ideal others, and an ideal family. This has made your life extremely difficult. The ideal self you think about is the perfect child, the perfect spouse, the perfect friend, the perfect parent. Since the fantasy cannot exist, you spend a lot of time judging yourself, because life doesn't work the way you decide it should.

In discovering what feels O.K., what doesn't, and why, you also need to take a look at this in terms of the way your family functions. It is now time for your family to learn how to solve problems and how to resolve conflicts. There are many ways to accomplish these things.

The first one is rather simple. Pick up a book on child development, so that you can learn what is expected at different stages. Because you did not develop like most children, you may be unnecessarily concerned about your children. Such a book will teach you what to expect at various ages. This is not an attempt to mold your children according to stages, but to gain a sense of whether or not they are somewhat predictable. This knowledge will give you a sense of security.

Along with that, you might also take a course in parent-effectiveness to learn the skills and techniques for comfortably relating to children. Remember, you are not expected to know all the answers. You are there with a lot of other people who care about their children, and want to develop better ways of communicating with them.

Barry and Aviva Mascari, who work with chemically dependent families, have developed an adaptation of the Adlerian family meeting. On a weekly basis, the family sits down and discusses the issues important to them, such as how much allowances should be, where to take the family vacation, and who is responsible for doing the laundry and taking out the garbage. This doesn't mean that your children take over the running of the family. It just means that all members of the family participate in the decision-making, so that there are no giant secrets. Everyone is considered, and no one is invalidated.

Much of your experience in growing up was that of being invalidated. You had the feeling that life would be better if you were out of the picture. It was a feeling that what you thought and said was not important. A first step in turning these feelings around, the family meeting will also make your children feel that their input is valuable. As a result, they will not have the feelings of invalidation that you had.

Something else you can do to discover what will work is to find a person you can talk to about anything. Have at least one person in your life with whom you do not have to worry about how stupid you might sound, to whom you can admit not knowing, to whom you can feel free not to even know the right questions to ask. A person like this is a treasure. I recommend that this person not be the adult child of an alcoholic, because there is a possibility that he or she is struggling with the same things that you are.

It is important to be able to risk admitting that you don't know. Owning up to not knowing something in a group of people always elicits the response: "I'm really glad you said that. I didn't know that either." But there is always one person in every group of people who says, "You don't know *that?*" You can learn to laugh at that remark, to discount it completely. Instead, use the support of those who are willing to learn and explore and not worry about having all of the answers all of the time.

I encourage you to trust your own instincts, which much of the time tell you the most appropriate way to behave. You tend to pull yourself back too quickly and decide that your instincts are not valid. By starting to trust them, you will soon learn that your instincts are a very valuable tool in developing the kind of healthy realtionships you want.

A client of mine told me how several people had gone to a lot of trouble to give her a special surprise party for her fortieth birthday. Her 20-year-old daughter was completely obnoxious. My client said, "You know, I really wanted to let her have it in front of all those people, but I held back." I said, "How come? That's what I think she deserved." My client said, "Well, I will next time. First I wanted to check it out with you."

This incident illustrates how to deal with a difficult situation. When something makes you uncomfortable, identify it. Talk about it and then make the decision about what to do. Situational issues can often be solved rather simply and easily. But those relating to the past are much more complicated.

Sandra is struggling hard with giving up the idea that she has to be the perfect parent and her children test her constantly. Her youngest child started a paper route. When the woman who gave him the route, who happens to be a fabulous Italian cook, said to him, "Can I pay you for this?" he said, "How about a hot meal?"

Sandra feeds her children, yet she became very upset and distraught because her neighbor might think she did not feed them. She had no sense of humor about the incident, nor did she know how to handle it. Her son was also having a breakfast of pancakes at another home, in addition to a full breakfast and dinner at home. Sandra needed to take a look at what caused her extreme discomfort. It had to do with her perfectionism, with the way she wanted to be seen in the neighborhood.

Another part of it was that she felt her son was taking advantage of her neighbors. That was the part that she could deal with, and so she called up the neighbor with the paper route. The neighbor thought it was quite funny and said, "That's quite a little boy you got there. I love to watch people eat. Feeding people is one of the greatest joys of my life. I know that he comes to my house directly from your house, but if you don't mind, I enjoy doing this for him."

Sandra felt relieved and they continued to talk. She admitted to this neighbor, who was also a friend, that her biggest concern was that she would think she did not feed her children properly. Her neighbor started to laugh, because even as the conversation took place, her neighbor was in bed running a high fever and feeling very guilty that she was absent from her graduate classes. She was not being the perfect student, and Sandra was not being the perfect mother, and both of them were feeling guilty. Discussing their problems made them feel better, because they became a little more realistic. This was important because being perfect is not realistic, and attempting to be perfect causes a great deal of anxiety. One can strive towards certain goals, but the goal of perfection does not have rewards in it that are beneficial.

A fully-functioning person knows how to handle conflict in a responsible manner. This includes how to confront, how to deal with, and how to resolve conflict. When you were growing up, you did not learn how to resolve problems. Problems were avoided, not resolved. As an adult, you still behave in ways that are not useful in this area.

Take this simple little test. Imagine that you are walking down a hall. There is a door in the hallway. You are about halfway down the hall, and coming out of that door is someone you are very angry at, or someone that you know to be angry at you.

What do you do? Do you stand your ground and confront that person and say, "It's good to see you. There are things we need to discuss." Or do you turn around and walk away? Do you make some frivolous remark that has nothing to do with what you two need to work out? Do you walk on and pretend he is not there?

What is it that you do when a potential conflict arises? How do you handle yourself? What is your initial reaction? To resolve conflict, you need to understand what you do and what goes on inside of you. This is a place to begin. Once you know that, you can make decisions about how you are going to deal with the problem and learn how to confront reality. Not really wanting to confront reality is the biggest issue in an alcoholic home. It is time to confront reality, and realize there is no such thing as normal. There is only reality, which you determine for yourself with the help and input of people who are interested and willing and anxious to participate in your development—thereby participating also in enhancing their own.

2. Adult children of alcoholics have trouble following a project through from beginning to end.

It is time for you to find out whether you are the procrastinator you think you are, or whether you simply lack information about how to complete a task. How does one follow a project through from beginning to end? How does that happen? It can, it does, and it will. It has to be done very systematically. People who carry projects through to completion don't do it casually. They have what we call a "game plan." They may have developed it to the degree that it looks automatic, but it is not. There is a process involved.

In the beginning, you need to be very aware of what the process is so that you can follow it, and so that you do not get stuck along the way and begin to judge yourself. The first thing you need to do when you conceive the project is to take a look at the idea. Is it manageable? Is it possible to accomplish what it is you would like to accomplish?

You then need to develop a step-by-step plan in order to accomplish it. You need to set a time limit for each step. How long is it going to take you to do each part of your project? You don't need to know exactly how long it's going to take, but you need to have a sense of what all of the parts are, and how much time you need to give to each part.

Once you have made that decision, the next step is to plan how you are going to meet the time limit. Is it realistic for you to do this project within this time limit, if all of these parts take this much time?

In developing the way you are going to meet the time requirements, you need to take a look at your own working style. The best way to do this is to reflect back on your learning style. When you were in school, how did you learn best? Were you the student who did best by doing a little each day, or by cramming the night before? Did you cram the night before because you learned best that way, or because there was no alternative? What ways were you most satisfied with what you were able to do? Study your own learning style.

If those steps don't fall into place and the goal isn't manageable, rethink the idea. Perhaps your idea was not realistic. If not, be willing to revise it. Perhaps you have taken on something more than you can do at this time. Or perhaps you need to approach the same idea somewhat differently. Be willing to revise the idea or the time limit. It may be that the idea is just fine, but you have not set aside enough time to accomplish it. Be willing at each stage to rethink and re-assess. See if there are changes that might occur along the way that will make a difference. You need not get stuck along the way because you have not figured out how it is going to be accomplished.

An example of this process should make it clearer to you. Paul is 48 years old and a very successful businessman. To a large extent, his business involves high pressure situations such as 24-hour time limits on preparing major reports. He goes from crisis to crisis, and does it extremely well. Crisis is something that he, as an adult child of an alcoholic, understands extremely well. He has used this aspect of his history to his advantage.

Paul decided that he wanted to get a Ph.D. After being accepted into a doctoral program, he came to me in a state of panic. "I cannot do this," he said. "It is not possible for me to do this dissertation." I smiled. He was overwhelmed at the project taking over a year to complete. Because he had no frame of reference for that kind of thing, he was scared. He is also intelligent enough to recognize that he was getting in his own way, and needed help to overcome the problem.

The first thing we decided was that he had to limit whom he talked to about it, because he was getting too much imput, too many different approaches. This, plus not developing his own approach, increased his anxiety. I simply said to him, "If I am going to help you, I am the only one to increase your anxiety at this time."

He also had the idea that his would be the most definitive dissertation of all time. He had to give up his grandiose notion and decide to research a subject that was manageable. He also had to name a committee of people whose input was pertinent and who wanted his project to be a success.

As soon as he did this, his panic started to subside.

The next step was to determine how long it would take to write the dissertation. He was in a panic as if it had to be done yesterday. The paper was going to take a year. It was going to take time to accumulate, assemble, and assess the material. It was also going to take time to interpret the results and write the paper in a way that would be acceptable to the members of his committee. It could not be done yesterday, and it could not be done tomorrow. A year was the only realistic assessment of how long the project would take.

Once that was understood, we could take a look at his learning style. How did he learn best? Could he do this the way he had done other things in life? It became clear that he could not do this the way he did other things, in a cramming, last-minute way. In addition, he did not want to take a month or two off work to work exclusively on the dissertation. It was decided that he would work two hours a day.

We also needed to look at what this meant. Did it mean that he had to write two hours a day? Or sit at his desk for two hours a day? Could he think during this time? The conclusion was to do something related to the dissertation during those two hours. The time spent thinking would later translate to time spent in writing. He need not be rigid with himself. We also determined that the place he worked best was at home at a little desk he had in the back room, where he could have some privacy. The most productive hours of the day were the first two hours in the morning. He would thus use the time before the rest of his family arose and before the phone started to ring.

These decisions were very basic and simple. But they made the difference between accomplishing and not accomplishing the task. And they were arrived at by very careful consideration.

Paul had never had the experience of planning out anything before. This was the first time someone had sat down with him and said, "How are you going to accomplish this? How are you going to get this done? What is your game plan? How long is it going to take? Is it feasible?"

After working on the dissertation for two weeks, he said he could not work two hours a day, but he could work one hour. This was by far more manageable for him, and he felt he could accomplish what he needed to in less time. This was fine. He developed a game plan and was able to revise it, once there was a structure which made the task more manageable. He was no longer in a state of panic which drained his energy and got in his way. He will now have less difficulty following a project through from beginning to end.

The steps outlined here apply to anything that needs to be accomplished. That wonderful idea that you have may or may not be possible. It does not come about through luck. It results through careful planning. As you have more experience with planning, you begin to do it automatically. The difficulty you have now may not be because you are procrastinating, but because you simply have not known about the process involved.

Your young children do not have to wait until they are adults to resolve this particular problem. If their teachers have been saying to you that they have not been living up to their potential, that they don't finish what they start, you can say, "My child needs to learn how to do it. My child may not be completing what he or she starts—not because she's not interested, not because she's not involved—but because we need to teach her how to do it." Sit down with the teacher, if he or she is sympathetic, and talk about how your child is going to develop the kinds of study habits that will make it possible to finish a project. Your children may not be doing as well as they would like to in school because they don't have the experience of seeing something begun and finished. This is no time to judge yourself and decide that you are a terrible parent. That will take energy away from helping your child and structuring the environment—a necessity for accomplishment. You can develop and organize a structure with or without the help of a teacher.

Guidelines need to be established. You don't need to be dictatorial; you can work them out with your children so that they become part of their life's design. They don't have to like it. It is time for them to begin to do things systematically. For example, homework should be done daily at a regular time and place for an agreed amount of time. This is the way to begin.

It is important to let them know they are not stupid, which they begin to believe very early on.

The difficulties result from lack of experience, but this is going to change. The family is going to enter into a partnership where they learn how to complete what they start. It is a process that everybody will be involved in, so they have more control of their lives. It will also improve your relationship with your children, and break the cycle in the next generation.

3. **Adult children of alcoholics lie when it would be just as easy to tell the truth.**

Lying is a very difficult habit to break, because when you were a child there was a payoff for not telling the truth. As an adult, there is no longer a payoff, but the habit persists. I have seen the habit broken mainly when the penalties are so great that life becomes unmanageable. The idea here is to stop lying before that happens. First, one must differentiate between the measured lie and the automatic lie. There may be a small payoff for you in a measured lie. It is not for me to judge; it is to give you a choice: to lie or not to lie. The cycle we are trying to break is the one where the lying is automatic and you have no control over it.

The initial step in overcoming any bad habit is becoming aware of it. If you have been lying automatically, you are not necessarily aware of what you have been doing. Promise yourself that you will not lie for one whole day. Then see what happens. You may or may not be able to do it.

If you can do it, fine. Was it easy or difficult for you? If you can't, write down what happened—what you lied about, and what was going through your mind right before you lied.

Assess what happened at the end of the day without judging yourself. You did what you did. You accomplished whatever you could accomplish. It was easy or it was difficult. You were able to do it for part of the day, but not for all of the day. You were able to do it in certain kinds of situations and not in others. Maybe you were able when you were relaxed and unable when you were stressed.

Just sit down and take a look at it. Rather than judging yourself, get to know yourself a little better by becoming a little more aware of how you behave.

Start the next day with the same resolve. Repeat the process. Do this for three or four days. At the end of that time, see what progress you have made. If you are still lying automatically, it's a good idea to make a commitment to yourself that the next time you find yourself lying, you will own up to it and correct any mis-statement you have made.

This is a powerful commitment. It means saying to yourself, "Even though the habit is strong, it is important to me that I change it." If you cannot do this, at least be realistic in accepting the fact that you are not ready to change, for whatever reason.

If increasing your awareness and accepting your commitment does not lead to the disappearance of automatic lying, it is probably more than just a bad habit. It may be something you need to work on at a deeper level. It may be a survival tactic, one whose time has passed. Because of your history and the childhood fears you developed, you may have to seek help to change your behavior.

Some things are resolved simply and easily. Others require a lot more work and assistance in their resolution. This is not to say that there is anything wrong with you. It may simply be more difficult for you than you anticipated.

When I work with someone who has a problem with lying, I say, "I believe that you believe what you just said." Then we can take a look at it, see what it means, and find out where the truth lies.

Many adult children of alcoholics go to the other extreme. Because there is so much lying, they resolve never to tell a lie. This is a more unusual way of dealing with that problem of growing up. It's a denial of the family pattern.

If you have been involved in the A.A., Al-Anon or Alateen programs, you can use their tools of recovery for breaking this habit. You can do what one does with alcohol. You commit yourself to stop drinking, and, one day at a time, you stop. One day at a time, you believe in yourself. One day at a time, you can work to change any bad habit you have.

4.   Adult children of alcoholics judge themselves without mercy.

Tim, a child of two alcoholics, wrote to me about himself and his feelings. He expressed his most significant discovery very simply: "Although I may make mistakes, I am not a mistake." These words show that he had achieved a certain amount of freedom. He had begun to look at himself honestly without judging himself. When one can separate the behavior from the person, one is free to change, develop and grow.

Although you have been told since childhood all of the ways you did not measure up, it is important for you to recognize that every statement has a positive and negative side to it. For example, if you are intelligent, that is wonderful, because you can understand things that less intelligent people cannot. Yet, these things are often disconcerting. If you feel deeply, the joy is greater than the pain. Who is to say what is good? Who is to say what is not so good? The idea is just to explore it, become fascinated by it, and see what it means.

You may have decided that your life is a Greek tragedy. I have a client who has done this, although there is very little evidence that anything other than her attitude is causing her problems. Life does not have to be perceived in various degrees of misery. If you perceive it this way, you might want to figure out what the payoff is. What do you gain by judging yourself? Why do you never judge on the good side? Why do you never pick out those things that make you special and wonderful? What is your need to come down on yourself? The answer is probably simple. Misery is familiar, and you have learned how to deal with distress. Life going really well is unfamiliar to you, so you don't know how to manage it. It is not unusual for clients to find a kind of comfort in their poor self-image.

When things start turning around, when they start looking and feeling better, then life becomes unmanageable. It is not unusual for the progress to be sabotaged. Even with a warning, the need for the familiar often takes precedence. After all, your earliest influences are the most powerful ones.

An exercise that I do with my students shows that judgments, good or bad, are a function of the person who holds them. The group sits around in a circle. A decision is made to build a monster in the center of the circle. It is our opportunity to purge ourselves of any qualities, wholly or partially, that we no longer want to possess. If the qualities being discarded are ones that someone else desires, he can pick them up. We go back and forth in this fascinating game. A man decides that he wants to give up 90% of his procrastination, and it is hardly out in the center of the circle before someone says, "I will take 75% of that, because I am much too compulsive."

Someone else says, "I want to give up all of my guilt," and somebody replies, "I need to take a little of that on. I don't want to look at my responsibilities in terms of the impact it has on others." People look surprised as we go on. When one person says, "I am tired of being so sensitive. I am going to give up 60% of my sensitivity," another says, "I have been insensitive long enough. I think I need some of yours."

This exercise clearly shows that our traits need to be looked at and explored. To what degree are they useful to us? To what degree do they get in our way? Certainly, judging them and judging ourselves is not useful. Who is to say what is good and what is bad? Somehow, if you step back and decide that you are you, and that is O.K., you have a lot more choices in life.

The monster ends up being a mixture—a confused mixture. And just about the only things that all people agree that they want to throw into the center are extra weight and oppressive mothers-in-law.

Another aspect of judging yourself that needs work is your acceptance of compliments. How well do you accept them? Do you automatically throw compliments away? It has been my experience that if something goes wrong, you will take on all the responsibility for it. But when something goes right, you dismiss it with, "It just happened," or, "It was easy." You may call this humility, but it perpetuates your negative self-image. It does not allow you to give yourself credit for the things that you do well, so that you can begin to feel better about yourself.

You may choose to sound humble to others, but be very sure that you accept what is due you. Because something is easy for you does not mean it is unimportant. Yet, if you make a careless mistake, that does not make that mistake any less important.

Try to be aware of the things that you do well. Do not dismiss them. Use them to build on, to become a whole person. You needn't judge them, as they are just part of the complete human being that is you.

5.   Adult children of alcoholics have difficulty having fun.

It is the child in us that has fun—that knows how to play. Because the child in you has been repressed for a very long time, it needs to be discovered and developed. You need to be the child you never were.

A friend once presented, somewhat frivolously, a rent-a-kid plan. He said that there are certain things that adults like to do that are much more fun if you have a kid along. Fishing is one of them, and he wanted to adopt a little red-headed, freckle-faced kid to take along. At the amusement park, he also wanted to have a kid with him so that he wouldn't look foolish riding on the ferris wheel.

This man also likes to swing at the playground. You know what people say when they see an adult on the swings, or in the sandbox. But if you just happen to bring a kid along, you get a lot of credit, either for being a good parent or an interested adult. Children know how to have fun.

So if you want to learn, spend some time with a child who knows how to have a good time. Do some of those child-like things that you never tried. What fantasy did you have in childhood? What game did you want to play that you never played? Now is the time to begin to play.

The more confident you are, the less afraid you will be of looking stupid. You may need to learn how to relax and do nothing. Simply take time for yourself without deciding that each moment has to be spent productively. Ironically, you may have to plan it. Book it into your day so that you don't spend that time thinking about all the silly things you wanted to do that you never got around to. I can have a very good time, but I'm not good at initiating it. Because I can't think of things to do that will be fun, I spend time with people who can. Not surprisingly, they are not adult children of alcoholic parents.

However, I must admit that part of the fun is to bring some of you guys along. When you let go and are flabbergasted by the good time you are having, it increases the enjoyment for the rest of us. The "Aha!" of the first experience is something very precious to share with another person.

6.   Adult children of alcoholics take themselves very seriously.

One of the reasons you have so much difficulty having fun, in addition to lack of experience, is that you take yourself too seriously. In order to overcome this difficulty, you need to separate yourself from what you do. You need to separate yourself from your responsibilities, such as your job. You do not have to be what you do. The key is to take your work seriously because it is relevant and important, but not to take yourself seriously. It is not all of you.

A good way to begin separating yourself from your activities is to make a schedule. If your job is supposed to last from 9 to 5, leave at 5:00. Hanging around until 7:30 does not make you more productive; in the long run, it will impair your efficiency. It may also be a cop-out on life.

A client who did hospital volunteer work was very involved with the terminally ill. She was also a lay minister who gave the Eucharist to bedridden people. She spent a lot of time in service, and being very supportive to people around her. When she came to see me, she was pretty much on the road to being burned out.

She didn't want to give up her work because she thought it was important and productive. She also felt that it was a part of who she was. I tended to agree with her, so we needed to find a way for her to make it manageable, so that there would be time left over for herself.

She already knew what to do with the time she had for herself. She was an accomplished musician, enjoyed the theatre, was very athletic, and had many friends. She had worked out how to spend her leisure time, but somehow it was only talk.

What we did was set up a very flexible schedule. She decided that she was going to do this two days a week, spending her morning working and afternoon playing. This was a way that she could take her work seriously, but still have time for herself. She could now do all of the things she wanted to do.

You need to plan conscientiously in order to begin to separate yourself from your activities. It will not happen on its own. It does not seem to work when you say, "I'm going to cut down on the hours that I work. I'm going to be different." One needs to be more specific.

You need to have other things to think about, and other things to do, in order to have a whole life. Otherwise, you will become narrow and limited, making it a lot harder to play. It will also make you a less-interesting person. What are you doing for yourself? Or, more specifically, what did you do for yourself today?

7. **Adult children of alcoholics have difficulty with intimate relationships.**

This has many aspects to it. The first is that adult children of alcoholics simply do not know how to have a healthy, intimate relationship. Your fear of intimacy, of letting anybody in, gets in the way. Part of that fear is of the unknown. What is it? What does it consist of? Intimacy implies closeness. How do you get close? What are the ingredients in a healthy relationships?

Keep in mind that healthy relationships do not develop overnight. There are many elements involved in a healthy relationship, and all of them must be shared. When entering into a relationship with another person, it is important to offer your partner that which you would want your partner to offer you.

The degree of intimacy is determined by the degree of sharing— by how much each member of the partnership is willing to give. It is, in effect, a contract which is best served when understood and declared. Many contracts are implied, but you need to find a way to check it out.

Several ingredients are essential to a healthy relationship. They apply whether the other person is a lover, parent, child, friend, spouse, or even an employer or co-worker.

The form or degree, however, may change according to the nature of the relationship. There is no attempt in this list to specify order or significance. What is important is that all of these ingredients should be present, and there should be mutuality. If any of them are missing, one cannot sustain a healthy relationship with that person.

Once again, bear in mind that intimacy is determined by the degree to which partners are willing to work at each one of these criteria. In certain types of relationships, this is more important and more appropriate than in others.

As you read the list, you might want to explore each aspect with respect to your relationships with people. Are they all present? This will show why some of your relationships are working well and others not quite so well. If any of these ingredients is missing, there seems to be a hole in the relationship.

VULNERABILITY—To what degree am I willing to let down my barriers? To what degree am I willing to allow the other person to affect my feelings?

UNDERSTANDING—Do I understand the other person? Do I understand what s/he means by what s/he says or does?

EMPATHY—To what degree am I able to allow myself to feel what he or she feels?

COMPASSION—Do I have a genuine concern for the issues that cause the other person concern?

RESPECT—Do I treat the other person as if he or she is of value?

TRUST—To what degree and on what levels am I willing to let the other person gain access to the things about me that I don't want everybody to know?

ACCEPTANCE—Am I O.K. the way I am? Is my partner?

HONESTY—Is this relationship built on truth, or are there games involved?

COMMUNICATION—Are we able to talk freely about issues that

are important in the relationship? Do we know how to do it so we are understood, and the relationship goes forward because of the sharing?

COMPATABILITY—To what degree do we like and dislike the same things? To what degree does it matter if we differ in certain attitudes and beliefs?

PERSONAL INTEGRITY—To what degree am I able to maintain myself as well as offer to the other person?

CONSIDERATION—am I mindful of the other person's needs as well as my own?

These are the ingredients that people have shared with me as essential to a healthy relationship. These are the parts of which it is made.

The bottom line in a healthy relationship and the one premise upon which everything else is based is, "Am I seen and do I see the other person realistically? Am I able to see him for who he is? Is he able to see me for who I am?"

If you are not realistic, the attributes do not matter. They are neither relevant nor valid. The ability to be seen and to see the partner realistically, regardless of the nature of the relationship, is critical to its health. It is perhaps more critical than if you had a different history, because you will react in ways that are inconsistent with developing a good relationship.

If you are realistic, you and your partner can talk about and learn from problems which can bring you closer together. If the relationship is based on fantasy, it may not be sustainable.

For example, adult children of alcoholics are afraid of being abandoned. When a problem arises, they panic, so the problem hardly ever gets discussed. If you are with someone who needs space and you panic, it will be extremely destructive. Try saying to your partner, "I have a problem in that I panic when we have a conflict. It's hard for me even to look at the problem. I know that you react differently, but promise me that even if you're angry at my behavior, you will reassure me that you love me. That way, we may be able to get back to the problem."

In a healthy relationship, these reactions are discussed. They should be discussed ahead of time so that when they come up, they are seen for what they are. The discussion itself will take away some of the fear of abandonment. Then you can say, "Now what was the problem that we had before I panicked?"

In any relationship, many of the problems that come up have to do with one's relationship with oneself. They are often disguised as problems in the relationship, and can also cause problems in, and even destroy, the relationship. Let me give you some examples.

Cheryl is the adult child of two alcoholics. She is ending a ten-year bad marriage, and has a very loving relationship with a young man. It is the healthiest relationship she has ever known. One of the problems that she has is that he wants to touch her. He wants to hold her and be physically demonstrative, and she finds that she backs away from this. The touching is almost aversive to her, except periodically. It seemed that her reaction was an over-reaction, since he didn't seem to be an oppressive person. He was willing to give her whatever space she needed, along with time by herself.

He was not oppressive in his demand, but needed to touch and be touched as an expression of feeling for her. He had been brought up in a physically demonstrative family. Her negative reaction was causing great problems in the relationship.

Since it was clear that she was over-reacting, we needed to look at her history to find out why.

It happened quite unexpectedly, when her mother came for a visit. She came around noon, started to drink, and continued to drink all afternoon. As she became drunker and drunker, she made more and more demands on her daughter. "Please touch me. Please hold me. I need you just to hold me." Cheryl said, "I did as my mother had asked, but it turned my stomach. She has been doing that to me since I was a little child."

When she told me about this, it was pretty clear where her aversion came from. It was no longer a big, dark secret, and now we could begin to overcome it. She reported to Ivan what was going on. She needed to let him know that her reaction had nothing to do with him; it was a result of her being a child of an alcoholic. That eased the situation somewhat, and we can now begin to work on changing her reaction to Ivan. If they hadn't been able to talk about it, and had lacked the ingredients of a healthy relationship, especially the ability to see each other realistically, this problem might have ended the relationship.

Kelly, too, is working on a new relationship that she is determined will be healthy and good for both her and her partner. Kelly, a nurse, came into therapy with this as her primary agenda. The child of two alcoholics, she had never seen nor had a healthy relationship. And she felt that, if left to her own devices, she never would. Her friend, a doctor, seems to be a considerate and thoughtful person who is willing to work on building a good relationship, and who wants to share his life with her.

One night she said, "This is it. It is done. It is over. I am finished with him. I never want to see him again. I thought maybe we could make it, but now I know that it is simply no good."

"What happened?" I asked.

"Last Wednesday night," she replied, "we talked about going out to dinner, and I decided that I really could not do that because I really had to clean the house. Once I get an idea in my head, that's the end of it. I knew that if I went out to dinner, my mind would be on cleaning the house, and I wouldn't have a good time. So I said, 'I will see you tomorrow, but I am going to stay home and I am going to clean the house.' Then, an hour later, he stopped by with a bottle of Lestoil and some Chinese food. His statement to me was, 'I knew you had to eat anyway, and I thought I would help you clean the house.' Can you imagine such a thing?" she said. "I went right off the wall. I don't think I have been quite so angry in my life."

I said to her, "It sounds to me like he was being thoughtful. Sounds to me like he was looking to spend time with you, and didn't want to miss out on it."

She answered, "That's what he said. He said, 'I knew you had to eat anyway and I wanted to help you clean if you had to clean. I don't care what I do, as long as I spend time with you.' "

I told her I thought that was a wonderful thing for him to do. So we began to explore what made it difficult for her to accept his kindness. No one had ever said, "Let me help you out. Let me do this for you, just because I care about you." It was an experience that was foreign to her. As a young child, she went out begging on the streets, because it was the only way to keep her and her brother out of a children's shelter and the authorities from finding out that they were being neglected. Her friend's kindness did not fit her frame of reference, so instead of accepting it, she became angry.

After we talked about it, she was able to understand his point of view a little bit better. It is still very hard for her to accept his kindness, but she was able to explain her reaction, even though it didn't make much sense to him. It wouldn't be understandable to anyone who didn't know what it was like to be the adult child of an alcoholic.

A lovely young couple came to see me because of a problem they couldn't resolve. Once again, the fact that the wife was an adult child of an alcoholic was relevant. The man had a problem with high blood pressure. His high blood pressure was related to the stress from his job, which he planned to change, and was a condition that ran in his family. The medication that his doctor put him on had a lot of side effects, and he preferred not to take it. In order for him to get off the medication, it was important that he not repress feelings such as anger, so he started letting it out in ways which were not harmful. He closed the car windows and screamed at his boss or at the other drivers on the road. He had a tantrum when a window wouldn't open. His yelling was harmless to others, and healthy for him in maintaining his blood pressure at the necessary level.

His wife, however, reacted very badly. She said, "I wish he wouldn't do that. He's yelling in the car all the time. He's screaming around the house all the time. I know he's not going to hurt anybody, but even so, I just can't take it. I just can't live with it."

He decided that rather than do anything to upset or hurt her, he would stop his yelling. He was also reluctant to tell her that it was healthy for him to yell. She kept saying, "Don't be afraid to tell me what you feel." But there was very clearly a double message. Don't be afraid to tell me what you feel, as long as what you feel is what I want you to feel.

We took a look at it. What did it mean? She said, "I'm not afraid of him. I know he will not harm me. There is no question of that. I don't understand what it is." And all of a sudden she flashed back to a time when her alcoholic mother behaved the way her husband behaved. She was losing control, yelling and screaming, and banging on doors for no apparent reason. This was very frightening to a little girl, because her mother was her source of security.

When this woman heard her husband act out, she over-reacted, because of her experience as a child. Now that they know what it stems from, they have a better chance of coming to grips with it. They can talk about it, and resolve the issue.

One of the things that happens when couples care about developing healthy, intimate relationships is that once the process is started, it has its own momentum. They really begin to enjoy exploring themselves and each other, and they have a commitment not only to the relationship, but to the self, which becomes more and more special as time goes on. Couples that begin to work on these skills, even if they start out ready to call it a day, are able to develop worthwhile relationships. They begin to enjoy communicating with one another, recognizing that they simply had not known how to do it. This knowledge gives them what they need in order to grow together, offer more to each other, and develop more fully as individuals.

If you have sexual concerns about yourself, they result largely from lack of information. The remedy is not complicated. There are several very good books on the subject. *Our Bodies, Our Selves*, gives you a lot of very good information—very clearly and very frankly expressed. There are a lot of technical "How-To" books. Why don't you read them so you can become familiar with different techniques of lovemaking?

The physical relationship that you have with another person is based not only on the technical know-how you can easily acquire, but is an aspect of a larger relationship. The physical relationship is one form of communication. All of the characteristics attributed to an adult child of an alcoholic can affect the sexual relationship. How well a couple relate sexually is symptomatic of everything else that is going on in the relationship.

As you grow as a person, and are able to relate better on a variety of different levels, you will also be able to communicate sexually in ways that are more satisfying to you. The sexual relationship is just one part of the total picture. It fits into place as everything else fits into place.

Your confusions about sex roles, masculinity and feminity, and appropriateness of behavior toward the opposite sex, are issues that concern everybody. They are not exclusive to adult children of alcoholics. We are going through a time when the norms are very unclear. Traditional forms are gaining power, and the not-so-traditional is losing power. Even with that trend, just about everything goes. All of these norms are operating at the same time. So if you are confused, you are in very good company.

There was a time when the male role was very clearly defined and the female role was clearly defined. This was true in the workplace, in the home, and in the bedroom. This is no longer true, and the definitions are changing.

The only way to know for sure who you are is to find out what works for you. That is essentially the whole message of this book. Find out who you are, feel good about who you are, and be willing to act upon it. That way you will be whole. You will be healthy in all aspects of your life. And you will be free.

8.   Adult children of alcoholics over-react to changes over which they have no control.

On the surface, adult children of alcoholics appear to be very rigid people. They seem to want things their way and no other way. This may be true, in part, but there is more to it than meets the eye. The issues that seem very simple to adjust to for others are a big deal for the adult child of an alcoholic.

I remember Martha falling apart, because plans to go to the city fell through at the last minute when her friends chose to do something else. It was a very big deal. Joan burst into tears because someone was late. He was not very late, but just the idea of being late set her off. At one point, another adult child of an alcoholic had her phone disconnected unintentionally. She decided that she was being punished, which was devastating to her.

These things on the surface do not seem big. Yet, if you are reading this, and you are the adult child of an alcoholic, you know how big they are.

Yet, they are all over-reactions, which generally are related to one's past history. Something like this has happened many times before, usually in childhood. A seemingly inconsequential incident is like the straw that broke the camel's back. It brings back all the plans that were never carried out, the promises that were never kept, and the punishment that you could not relate to your crime.

This is what happens when plans to go to the city are disrupted, when someone is late, when the phone company inadvertently disconnects your phone. The pain you experienced a a child is experienced in the moment and *nobody, nobody* is ever going to do that to you again.

Coming to grips with this issue requires a great degree of self-awareness. The first thing that you have to do is recognize it when you over-react. You may be able to do that for yourself. Is your reaction inappropriate to the circumstance? Is somebody whose opinion you respect saying to you that you are over-reacting? Have you become irrational? Is the situation worth reacting to as strongly as you are reacting? What is your response when someone says to you, "Why is it such a big deal?"

If you become defensive with that question, then you have over-reacted. If you are not reacting in an appropriate way, you need to ask yourself, "What was the circumstance in and of itself that made it so big?" Why did it really matter to you that the change occurred without your helping to effect it? And what did that mean to you? When did it happen before?

Lack of awareness created the feeling that an injustice has been done deliberately against you. The extension of this kind of thinking is a paranoic attitude toward life. "They're out to get me, because they changed the plans at the last minute, or they were late, or they unintentionally disconnected the phone. They did it deliberately." This extreme attitude can develop if you don't understand that your over-reaction results from your history.

The first, and perhaps most significant, way to overcome this is to increase your awareness of over-reactions, and what has happened in your past that causes them. Another way to change is to deliberately change your normal routine. Take a look at the day. Are you rigidly locked into everything you do? Can you go home a new way? Is it possible to shop on Thursday this week instead of Wednesday? Can you shift things around without causing yourself a lot of turmoil?

You may find that it is harder than you think to break your routine. But it is a place to start being somewhat flexible. Flexibility in one area will generalize to other areas. You will probably be surprised at the degree to which you have settled into a routine, and how carefully structured your days are. You might, from time-to-time, throw it all up in the air and run in another direction, almost as if you are rebelling against yourself. But, in terms of the overall design, you probably are very routinized. Easing that up will help to ease you up, which will help you develop some freedom to affect the things you can, and to accept the things that you can't. This doesn't mean that you have to like everything that happens. You don't have to be the adult child of an alcoholic to be disappointed when a change occurs that you did not anticipate, or you did not want, but you do not have to be devastated by it, and that may be the difference. It does not have to affect your whole being.

9.   **Adult children of alcoholics constantly seek approval and affirmation.**

The issue here is one of self-confidence. There are a variety of ways to become more confident in one's own abilities.

The first way is concerned with the support and encouragement of other people. Adult children of alcoholics are constantly seeking that encouragement, but they don't seem to be able to use it. It is very hard to trust when you have been taught trusting will only offer you pain. It is very hard to trust when the messages you received as a child were very inconsistent. You were programmed not to trust, but to believe what is said is not necessarily what is meant. Adults did not say what they meant, nor did they mean what they said. This makes trusting extremely difficult. So when someone gives you support and encouragement, it is very hard for you to feel it, accept it, and use it.

So you continue to look for it, because it is so difficult for you to internalize. Only if you become bombarded with encouragement to such a degree that you can no longer deny it, will you begin to believe it.

So the first step is to decide that you are going to take the risk and allow some of the support and encouragement to be felt. Begin by identifying a few people whom you can trust. There are certain criteria that you might set up. How well does this person know you? Is it someone with whom you have a lot of contact? To what degree does this person accept you as you are? To what degree do they trust you? How much do you accept the other person? (This might make it easier for you to trust the other person's judgment.) Is this person an expert in the area in which they are offering you support and encouragement? These are the questions that people ask themselves when they are trying to decide whether or not they can use and trust someone's support and encouragement.

One young person who is not the child of an alcoholic said to me, "I do something very different. Support and encouragement are good energy. I take that energy and use it in order to be able to accomplish even more. I take those good feelings and use them in order to feel a little more. I like that." She didn't have to judge. For whatever reason when she was told, "Try it. It's a good idea," she decided, "Why not?"

While you are working on being more receptive to support and encouragement from others, you also need to work on building self-confidence. Here are some ways that you can begin.

Ask yourself what you did today that you feel good about. The answer to that will not come quickly or easily. Then ask yourself what happened today. Is there something, no matter how little or how simple, you can count as a little success? Go through the day. You didn't wake up as a grouch. That may be an achievement for you. You got to work on time. That may be something you don't do often. Whatever it is, don't throw it away. Don't throw away the credit for any little successes just because anybody can do it. You did it. It therefore is your success.

You need to continue to strive, giving yourself credit for whatever you accomplish. You will gain self-confidence if you accomplish the tasks that you set for yourself. They may be very simple tasks, or they may be big tasks, but commit yourself to accomplishing the task, once you recognize that it is realistic.

If you have a difficult task, practice rather than project disaster. If you are going for a job interview, don't waste your time in a state of panic. Practice by yourself. Practice with a friend, so that it will not be completely new to you when you go for the interview. Don't spend time projecting disaster or success. Spend your time in the present moment.

Not everything will work out. If it does, that's terrific. But it didn't just happen. You were responsible for the success. If it doesn't work out, then you will go out and try something new. It doesn't have to devastate you. You are not responsible for everything that doesn't work out, and everything that does work out is not a matter of coincidence.

Again and again, people will come into my office and say, "Things really went well," and they are astonished. I look at them and say, "It was no accident that it went well. You have been working on that for several weeks. You have been working very hard on having things go well. When they go well, it is a result of your hard work. Step by step. Little by little. It's not an accident that it went well."

These are some of the ways to build up self-confidence— by little successes, and by acknowledging the little successes. Little things that come easily for you are not without value. Build on the things that you can do well. Take it one step at a time, one day at a time. Begin to trust yourself and others. You never again will be in a position where you have no option but to trust those who cannot trust themselves. You now have a choice. You know better now who to trust. You know better now where you can trust yourself and where you can't trust yourself. You know where the help is. All you have to do is use it.

10. Adult children of alcoholics usually feel different from other people.

The feelings of isolation you had as a child make connection with other people extremely difficult. You longed for connection, but could not effect it. As an adult, these same feelings persist.

It is difficult, if not impossible, to wholly overcome these feelings, but there are ways of reducing the feelings of isolation. They may require some risk and some hard, but necessary, effort. First, you need to take the risk of sharing with others. This will help you to realize that although you are unique as a person, you are not all that different from others.

Find out all you can about what children of alcoholics feel like. This will help you to understand that you are not different. Intellectual understanding will not really change your feelings much, but it will make it a little easier for you to push yourself.

Joining a group will be helpful. It can be an adult children of alcoholics group, or any group of people that share their thoughts and feelings. Since not all of your feelings are related to your history, it may be helpful to learn which ones are and which ones are not. You will not find any group that does not have some adult children of alcoholics in it. You will never be the only one, yet this fact is not often shared.

When I talk about risk, I mean putting yourself out. The risk involves letting people know who you are and getting to know yourself better. The payoffs are getting to know others better, and starting to feel a little bit connected. Feeling alone in a crowd will begin to diminish.

The only way to get the things you really want is to give them away. If you need to be loved, offer love to others. I know if I need to be understood, the way to insure it is to offer understanding. The same is true if I want to feel close. The only way I know for sure that I can be close to another person is if I can allow that person to be close to me. If I can say (not necessarily aloud), "You can come in close. I'm not afraid of your coming in close. I will offer you myself, my friendship, my caring. I will offer you the things I need for myself, and this will help reduce the isolation for both of us."

I'm not sure one ever completely loses the sense of isolation. I'm not sure anyone with this kind of history ever feels wholly connected. But it is not only adult children of alcoholics who feel somewhat different from other people, and who do not feel a part of the group.

For example, if you are a professional or a boss, you will be isolated from those who work for you. They will be friendly to you, but you will not be one of them. Because you may be in a more prominent position, you will feel separated from the group. If you are in a helping profession, your clients will not connect with you as a person. They will see you as separate and apart, which they do for their own well-being.

If you are becoming self-actualized, if you are discovering who you are, and living your life on your own terms, you will also feel somewhat alienated. The only way to avoid this feeling is to make, from time-to-time, the decision to do it their way and accept the norms of the group you happen to be with. If you have decided to accept the norms of AA, you will probably feel a sense of connectedness at an AA meeting. This will also happen in a church group. You will not feel connected all the time, but you will feel connected when you have not made decisions for yourself that are different from those of the rest of the group.

It is important to select just a few special people in your life and offer them what you want, and they, in turn, can offer you what they want. Not taking the risk leaves you isolated. But taking the risk gives you the opportunity to change. Trying it once is not enough. Promise yourself that every day, in a very small way, you will reach out to another person, either by getting to know them better for who they are, or by letting them know you a little better for who you are. You will initiate the interaction and will try to accept that which is offered you.

11.   Adult children of alcoholics are super responsible or super irresponsible.

The issue here is the need to be perfect. "If I am not perfect, I am nothing. If I am not perfect, I will be rejected. I will be abandoned. I know that I am not perfect, but if I try hard enough, no one else will know. Therefore, I will be the perfect employee, the perfect spouse, the perfect parent, the perfect friend, the perfect child. I will always look perfect. I will always say the right thing. If I am perfect, my boss will love me, my parents will love me, my friends will love me. All I have to do is whatever I am asked, and more. All I have to do is everything. But please don't let them look under the rug!"

Can you feel the pressure from just reading that? It's enormous. The task to change is also enormous. If you are not the super achiever, but are the super irresponsible one, the task to change for you, too, is enormous, but it's much more easily expressed. The other side of the scenario goes, "If all that is true, why bother?"

They may or may not love you. People resent perfect people because they can't compete, but others love you if they love the image that you have projected. Of what use to you is the love? You have to continue to be stressed in order to hang on to it. If they love you and know the real you, chances are they won't run off into the night if you run downstairs with your hair in curlers.

Therein lies the risk. Many super responsible people, in order to stop, have to get sick. It is the only way out, and it is very predictable. They give and give, and take more upon themselves until they no longer have anything left, and they get sick. In effect, they burn out. They cannot find an acceptable way to stop short of this.

Eric is a perfect example. He is still in the process of recovering from a terrible auotmobile accident that happened two years ago. He's in a new marriage, with a new set of children, and new problems. He is beginning a new career and looking for a job.

Along with all this, he has invited his recently-widowed and very depressed mother into his home. He has decided to be responsible for the emotional care of a brother who is just getting out of a relationship, and for another brother who is trying to lick his chemical dependency, besides making sure that every whim of his mother-in-law is carried out. The statements I made in terms of relieving the pressure were countered with, "If I don't do it, who will?"

Eric reached the point where he simply could not do it anymore.

His body refused to get out of bed. To all the people in his life, he looked sick. He was sick, and it gave them an opportunity to be responsible. They took charge of their own lives, which gave him an opportunity to stop being such a super person. Yet, he had to get sick to do it.

The same is true with Paula, a divorced woman with an alcoholic mother who is still drinking. She has one child of her own, and has been involved with a father of five. Paula has a full-time job. She has also taken over the responsibility for her boyfriend's home and his children. This means that before she goes to work and takes her own son to school in the morning, she stops by another household and makes all of the lunches, does all of the laundry, and gets the five children off to school.

Paula had only been seeing me for a few weeks when she broke her foot. I told her it was no accident. The only way she could slow down, the only way that she could stop proving herself, was for something to happen that incapacitated her. Not surprisingly, her lover is quite angry that she hurt herself, and she is now looking at the relationship a lot more closely. Her mother now has a reason not to drink for awhile, so she can play mother. And Paula can begin to find ways to become somewhat less responsible.

In order to help these two people start living realistic lives, it was necessary to give them very specific guidelines. In Paula's case, it was easy. Her son broke out with a very serious rash. She promised me that she would not consider going back into the relationship with her boyfriend until her son's skin cleared up. This contract allowed her to begin to change.

In Eric's case, his family became very concerned about his health, and promised they would help him and find the strength that they had within themselves all along to become adults and confront their own problems. He had become just too convenient for everyone. That has now changed.

In both cases, somebody took over and was supportive. It may not always happen this way, but unless you give others a chance, there is no chance that it will.

You do not have to wait until you are in such an extreme position to begin to work on the problem. A part of your difficulty may lie in not realistically assessing your own capabilities. You may not have assessed what is fair for someone else to ask of you. Perhaps you may not have learned how to delegate responsibility.

Looking first at your work, you need to set up some specific guidelines for yourself. How late am I willing to work? When is it time to quit and go home? Check it out with others. What do they do? What is your job description? What is expected of you in this position? What can be asked of you? What is reasonable? What is fair? How much responsibility is yours and how much responsibility of the work belongs to somebody else? What is workable and what isn't workable? These things really need to be looked at very carefully. You may also need to discuss them with another person.

One of the most outrageous circumstances that I've encountered involved a woman who had gone home from work because someone very close to her was dying. While she was sitting in the hospital's intensive care unit, her boss called and told her to return because of a deadline. Since she was the child of two alcoholics, she didn't know what was appropriate and came back. Needless to say, I was flabbergasted. She simply did not know the answer to the question, "Do I really have to do that?"

When someone asks you to do something, ask yourself, "Do I really have to do it? Do I really want to do it?" The answer may not always be "no," but "no" is an option that is always available to you.

When I was in Israel one summer, I was touring with a group. It was 115 degrees and they started climbing up a mound to see Jerico, which is just a pile of ruins. I started to climb with them, then stopped and said, "Hey! I don't have to do that!" They looked at me in great surprise, and another woman on the tour said, "You know, you're right. I don't have to do that either!" They never forgot that. Later on in the tour when we were in a cable car climbing up Masada, she turned to me because she had a fear of heights and said, "Do I have to do it?" Since we were halfway up the side of the mountain, there was no choice.

"Do I have to do it?" is a question you need to ask yourself. If you're not sure, discuss it with someone you can trust, not someone who has a vested interest in your completing the task.

The next step is for you to learn to say "No," if that is your decision. This is very hard to do. It involves practice and it involves taking a risk. People may not like it when you say "no" and accept saying "no" as part of who you are. Look at the possible consequences and be ready to handle them. Is it worth it, and what is your motive in saying "no?"

It may be that you don't want to jump right into saying "no." You may not want to do this as compulsively as you have done other things. Instead, you might decide to buy time with "I can't make a decision right now. let me get back to you." If they want an immediate decision, then you can say, "I need time to think about it."

Giving yourself time to think should make it easier to say "no" if that's how you feel. It will also give you an opportunity to figure out an alternative. Buying time can enable you to make a responsible decision and everybody will be satisfied.

If you think about it, and part of your message to yourself (since you are such a super achiever) is, "Maybe I can fit it in," the next question to ask yourself is, "Do I want to?" That may be the key. "Do I want to? Or is there something I would rather do with my time?" Maybe you would rather do nothing. That can be as important for you as anything else, if you choose it because you want to do nothing, not because you've reached the point where you no longer have the energy.

Being super irresponsible can result from one of two things. The first is that you chose never to get started, and the second may be because you burned out. Although the results of these two look similar, they are very different, and they need to be looked at differently. If you have burned out, you need time to rest and recover. You may need to opt out for a while. There's nothing so terribly wrong with that. You need time to regroup, to heal, before you can go forth again. However, the next time you get up the energy, you may need to live in a more measured way.

In recovering, you need to begin giving to yourself. You probably need to learn how to do this. Think about the things that make you feel good. You might go to a burnout clinic and find out the specific ways people use to recover. You need to begin to learn how to take in energy, not only to give, but to get.

Take a look at the people in your life, at the nature of your relationships. Are you getting to the degree that you are giving? Have you surrounded yourself with people with strength to offer you as well as your offering to them? It may be that if you look around carefully, you will discover that you are involved with a population that is drawing from you, but giving nothing. You may need to change this by developing relationships with people who have as much to offer you as you have to offer them. It may also be that you have not allowed the people around you to offer to you. You have been playing super strong, and now is the time to let others help you so that you can regain your strength.

This time you need to do it more realistically, not being all things to all people all of the time. You now see that the payoff is not worth it. Martyrs are rarely appreciated in their lifetime.

Super responsible people tend to be exploited. Somehow they almost demand it. So this time, when you look at what you plan to do for your life's work, make sure that you do not get exploited. Find out if you are being paid what the job is worth. Find out all you can.

Jen did this, and once she found she could not work in such conditions, she confronted her boss. She had decided she would prefer to lose the job than allow herself to be exploited. It worked out well for her. Her employer gave her what she considered reasonable. It does not always work out so well, but your self-respect may be worth it.

If you are super irresponsible and it does not result from being burned out, but from never having gotten started, the problem is somewhat different. Your decision to read this book probably means you are ready to change. This is a difficult problem. You may need to find out what it is you want to do. You may have to begin in a direction and start by having little successes. You may want to do some testing and find out what vocational areas are of interest to you. You may think about going to school. It will probably be a good idea to do this with some professional direction—to work out a plan with someone who understands what is happening to you psychologically, and how difficult it is for you to become more responsible, and to become less afraid of success and all that it implies. This may be something you cannot do alone. You can certainly begin. But if you find yourself becoming paralyzed at the moment things begin to work for you, you may find—as one of my clients found—he could go so far and no further. He found he could get up to the college campus, but not go to the registrar's office. He could fill out the application forms, but he couldn't make it for the interview.

Check out how far you can go alone, but this may be something you will need help with. It doesn't mean that you are sick. It just means that this is a hurdle that you need professional help in order to overcome. The decision to do so is probably the hardest part.

12. Adult children of alcoholics are extremely loyal, even in face of evidence that the loyalty is undeserved.

Loyalty is a very admirable quality. Yet any quality that is extreme may not be beneficial to you. You are indiscriminately loyal to all those who come within your circle and touch your life. Your loyalty extends to lovers, to friends, to family, and to employers. To have you in any of these relationships is extremely valuable. And your fears of being abandoned make it almost impossible for you to abandon others.

If you are involved with people who are not treating you as you need to be treated, it is important to rethink your loyalty. It may not be appropriate. You do not automatically owe loyalty. The relationships I'm talking about are the ones where you say to yourself day after day, "Why do I bother? Why do I stay with it? Is it worth it? Why am I such a fool? Why can't I let go?"

To overcome a tie that you no longer desire, there are a number of steps you can take. The first is to specify the reality of the situation. Ask yourself, "What is the nature of this relationship? What is going on at the moment?" Then you will hear yourself begin to say, "But, but ..." When the "buts" start, you are no longer in the moment. You are no longer in the reality, but into a fantasy of the past or a fantasy of the future. "Why can't it be like it was?"

It can't be like it was, because it is no longer like it was. You need to understand what the difference is. In the initial stages of reality of a relationship, people often treat each other differently than after it becomes a part of the routine. You may not do this, but others might. And you find yourself assuming that if he or she is no longer treating you as in the beginning, then there is something wrong with you. "If I could only do or say the right thing, life would be as it was." That is not realistic.

As a relationship develops, and the people get to know each other better, the relationship has to change. It can become more meaningful or less meaningful. People can become more considerate or less considerate. Many things happen. Nothing stands still, so what existed in the beginning no longer exists.

The fantasy that if you can just get through a difficult time, things will be wonderful, may not be realistic.

Living in the future is not a good idea, because the future cannot be predicted. When couples in healthy relationships go through difficult times, they share their feelings with each other. If they take out their aggressions, they talk about it and how to prevent its happening again.

How much energy you put into a relationship is an important consideration. When you start to back off, to want more equality in the relationship, very interesting things start to happen. If you look back realistically at what happened in the initial stages of a relationship, you may find that you put an awful lot of energy into it. This is your way, and you enjoy doing it.

The other person responded. And then somewhere along the line, you may have felt a need yourself. You may have withdrawn a little bit of energy, and the other person didn't like it. This may be the time when s/he stopped treating you the way you wanted to be treated. This may be the point at which you started to become unhappy—when you withdrew a little bit, and s/he was no longer riding on your energy.

I know a man in a situation like this. When the woman, who was an adult child of an alcoholic, withdrew some energy, people started to see him as shorter. She had given so much to him that when she slowed down, he literally looked shrunken.

The first step in deciding whether or not your loyalty is appropriate is to be realistic about what the relationship consists of. Do not allow yourself to live in the past or future projection. The present is what is real. Ask yourself, "What is best for me now? Is my loyalty to the person I know in the moment?"

A certain amount of loyalty is appropriate if the relationship is with a child who is going through a terrible stage, or if the relationship is with someone who is very ill and cannot offer what they offered at one time. You might want to remain loyal, but need to make this a conscious decision. You may need to say, "I care about Janine. I'm going to stay with her. I will be loyal to her, even though she is not good for me right now. I will be careful. I will protect myself, in the hope that this will be resolved."

The next thing that you need to do if you want to make decisions about loyalty, and not have it be automatic, is to begin to say to yourself, "What is in this for me? What is the payoff? Why do I maintain this relationship? Who is this other person to me?" The answers to these questions are often quite surprising. You may find that a person represents someone else in your life. Your lover may be very much like your alcoholic parent was when you were growing up. You may be repeating a pattern, because it is familiar. You may not have broken early ties, and are setting yourself up again.

How is that person like you? Have you been drawn to someone who is very much like yourself? Who is that person? What does that person represent to you?

After you have the answers, you need to begin separating yourself from the other person. Begin to acknowledge where the other person ends and where you begin. Differentiate between what has to do with her/him and what has to do with you. When this is clear, the other person's hold on your feelings will decrease.

The people who are undeserving of our loyalty quite often are very critical of us. They spend a lot of time telling us what is wrong with us. Be careful when you hear this. If you decide to listen, be sure who the other person is really talking about. Do his/her statements really have to do with you, or is s/he merely projecting him/herself on you? Be mindful of where the other person ends and you begin. Another's pain, sorrow, or anger belongs to them. You may be compassionate and empathic, but it is not yours. The loyalty where you lose yourself and become submerged into another person is not in your best interest.

You may get hooked through guilt into a relationship that is not good for you. If you are easily manipulated by guilt, you think you owe the person something. When I ask my clients what they owe, I hear, "Well, s/he was nice to me. Well, s/he cared about me."

You become guilty and feel that you owe for the wrong reasons. If someone cares about you, it is because you are worth being cared about. Your friendship is a gift. You are under no obligation to someone, just because they befriended you. You are of value. If you owe them because they befriended you, you are saying, "I am not of value." When you begin to back away, the other person will try to make you feel guilty. S/he will talk about how much s/he wants you, and needs you, and you will find it very difficult to break away.

This may be a time when the relationship can change. You can say, "I don't want to end this, but I can't continue in a relationship that isn't good for me. If we can talk about it, and if it can change so that it can be good for both of us, maybe I will think about it some more."

To stay in a relationship out of guilt is something you have to look at carefully. Your friendship is a gift. It is to be cherished. It is not something that you owe because somebody accepted it from you. Take a good, hard look at what you have offered, and what has been offered to you. Do you still feel that you need to be indebted? Have you looked at it fairly and realistically? Swallow that but, but, but ...

You may also continue in relationships that are not good for you because you are afraid of being alone. You have a fear of loneliness and isolation. This is probably not your last opportunity to have a friend or a lover, or the only person in the world who will ever care about you. You may have made this somewhat bigger than it is. Remember, you have yourself. Isn't that glorious? It can be, if you get to know yourself. This fear of being alone with yourself can be turned into a desirable experience.

You may also be staying in a relationship because it makes you feel superior. If your partner does not offer you all that you can offer, you can feel more important and feel that s/he should be indebted and loyal to you. In effect, you are saying, "The only way I can feel good is to be involved with someone who is less than I am. This way I can build my ego. If you are lower than me, I can elevate myself."

This may be the payoff. "Although you don't treat me as I need to be treated, I feel superior, and that is a way I falsely build my self-esteem." This is something you may need to look at very carefully. Even though you complain, is there something about it which gives you pleasure?

You may sincerely think that you are in love with someone, and I would never argue about that. If I were to define it, I would define love as enhancement. If you and I are in a loving relationship, we enhance each other. We are more than we would be if we were not involved. That is probably where your loyalty is inappropriate— even if you call it love.

What you did call it may not be very important. The important question is, "Is it good for me?" It's very much like discussing whether you're an alcoholic. I won't enter into that discussion either. I don't know if you're alcoholic, but why don't you just not drink? I don't know if you love this person, but why don't you just decide that nobody has the right to treat you less than well, because you love yourself and because you are important to yourself.

If you decide that you need to change a relationship, and that your loyalty is best offered elsewhere, it may be hard for you to break away completely because of your fears. Why limit yourself? Why not develop other friendships? Why not put your energy into those, and try to be more realistic with them. As those relationships develop, you can begin to diminish the one that is not good for you. It does not have to be all or nothing. You may not have to eliminate this person completely, but simply lessen the impact of the relationship. There are many choices and many directions. Being realistic about who and what you want is the place to begin.

13. Adult children of alcoholics tend to lock themselves into a course of action without giving serious consideration to alternative behaviors or possible consequences. This impulsivity leads to confusion, self-loathing, and loss of control of their environment. As a result, they spend tremendous amounts of time cleaning up the mess.

The impulsive behavior we are discussing is not unlike a two-year-old who has a temper tantrum because he wants what he wants when he wants it. The toy he has his eye on is the only thing that is important in his world. It is not unlike the two-year-old who decides to run across the street in the middle of heavy traffic.

A two-year-old will also hold his breath until he turns blue. Because he wants attention so badly, he will punish himself by hurting himself. Your behaviors are not much different. The main difference is that you are the one who is held responsible for these behaviors. The two-year-old has someone else to hold responsible. It is quite possible that in a different environment, you might have developed differently, and your desires would now affect you differently.

But that's not the issue here. It is what you are going to do so that you don't behave like a two-year-old. You know that it can't work for you, which may be the only thing that separates you from the child.

The key here is to head you off at the pass, get in the way of your impulses until you have examined what the consequences and the alternatives are. It it important to slow you down, so that once locked in a course of action, the key is not thrown away.

If you are working with a counselor, or if you have a sponsor whom you speak to on a regular basis, you may be able to buy a little time. The following examples show how the problem was resolved for my clients.

One female client had many disastrous relationships with men.

We began to look at just exactly what was happening. What was she contributing? Who was she selecting? We were beginning to look at all the issues involved, and decided that she could not be considered a victim.

She called me one afternoon right before I was leaving on a business trip and said, "I have discovered the answer. You and I have been looking in the wrong place. It is not that I have problems with relationships. I have problems with men. I think the truth is that I would have a much easier time if I were involved with a woman, and I think that is what I am going to do. I met this woman, and that is a new direction for my life."

The thought that went through my head was, "What can I do to slow this down?" The sex of the person involved is not the point. If you can't relate to a male, you can't relate to a female. And it certainly would have made her life a lot more complicated to enter into a homosexual relationship.

My answer was, "Could you wait until I get back from my trip?" She agreed, which was reasonable. If this was, in fact, the direction for her life to take, waiting a week or two would make no difference. It turned out that was all the time she needed. By the time I returned, it was no longer even something she wanted to discuss. It was over. The impulse of the moment had passed.

A similar thing happened with Harold. He called to tell me that he hated his boss, and his job, and that he was in the wrong field. He had written a letter of resignation which he planned to give his boss in the morning.

I suggested that he wait until we looked over the letter together. He agreed to do that. It wasn't all that urgent. It had to be done very shortly, but it certainly didn't have to be done the following morning. He agreed. By the time that he came in three days later, his position had changed. He was no longer quite so angry, and his sense of urgency was gone.

These are two circumstances where the people were aware enough to know that maybe they were on the wrong track. There was a chance that the behavior they thought very rational and reasonable in the moment might cause them stress later on. It's more usual for me to hear what someone did last night than what they are going to do tonight.

If you are not receiving professional help, there are ways that you can begin to overcome impulsivity yourself. You will recognize that impulsivity, because there is a lot of energy involved. You will recognize it, because you will feel driven, impelled, and you can think of nothing else.

When you get that feeling, say to yourself, "Who else is going to be affected by this behavior?" I'm not suggesting to you that you say, "This is good," or "This is bad," or "This is poor," or, "I shouldn't do this," or "I should do this," because, in the moment, this is the only way that you see it, and it really doesn't matter whether you like or dislike it. It's the only way.

What you need to do then is to look at the other people involved in this behavior. Who else is going to be affected by what I do? How are they going to be affected by what I do? You may not care how you are going to be affected at a time when the action seems to take over. Your sense of yourself seems to be lost, although you think that you are experiencing yourself fully.

Asking yourself those two questions should be enough to delay the action. Delaying the action will give you time to look at the consequences and the alternatives.

A decision made impulsively might not always be bad for you. Quitting a job could be the best thing that you can do for yourself. It might be that homosexuality is preferable for you. But these decisions should be made after consideration of the alternatives and consequences. They should be made with a clear mind, so that you will be certain you are comfortable with what you are doing. Then you won't have to say to yourself, "I wish I hadn't acted so rashly."

Perhaps what is good for you is not good for the other people around you. Considering them may be important too. Quitting your job because you hate your job may be good for you. Yet, if you are the sole support of dependent minors, it's not an appropriate move. If you believe that many of your problems are caused by trying to be straight and you are married, acting out in the moment could be damaging to your spouse.

I am not telling you what decision to make. I am suggesting that you find a way to buy time, so that you consider the implications of your actions. Here, as in every other aspect of your life, choice is important. If you make a conscious active choice and are willing to be held accountable for your behavior, you will feel much better about yourself, regardless of the choice you make.

Your life experience has been such that if what was promised didn't happen immediately, it simply didn't happen. Now that you are not living in the same environment, however, the rules can change. Look back at the things you did so quickly, and at the gratification that you had to have in the moment. What was in it for you to do it that quickly? Was it to your advantage in the short run? Was it to your advantage in the long run?

For example, many of you quit school. What did you gain? What do you regret most about the things that you did too quickly? The things you regret may have been the things you thought you wanted in the moment. You need to begin taking a broader look at your life.

One of the ways to do it is to fantasize. Where would you like to be in five years? Do you want to be doing what you're doing now? Do you want to take a different direction in your life?

Think out the necessary steps to get there. When you look at those steps, you will see all of the gratification is not at the end. For example, in studying for a degree, you don't get all of the gratification the day you get the diploma.

There are many little gratifications along the way. Think about that. Build in those gratifications. Build in your own reward system. When the elementary school teacher gave out gold stars to the children who handed in good papers, it served a purpose. It said, "You did this well." No situation is an all or nothing proposition.

When you do things too quickly, you sometimes ask the wrong questions, or make the wrong decisions. "I want a divorce" may mean "I don't want to live like this." These are very different statements. The decision "I don't want to live like this" can change into "I'm NOT going to live like this." It does not necessarily mean divorce.

It may mean a change of lifestyle. It may mean going into counseling, or many other things. It may also mean divorce, but not necessarily. If you defer the gratification, you will have an opportunity to find out what it really does mean. You might be feeling stifled. That doesn't necessarily mean divorce. It probably means making some new decisions with respect to your life.

I'm not going to pretend that the gratification you wait for is always more wonderful that what you decided in the moment you wanted.

That would be foolish and unrealistic. Sometimes deferred gratification is more wonderful and the experience is richer, but it does lack the excitement of doing what you want when you want to do it.

The problem with immediate gratification is not how it feels in the moment. It feels great in the moment. Walking out of school and knowing you never had to face your geometry teacher again felt super. That gooey, gooey dessert you ate last night tasted delicious. That person you went to bed with in a moment of extreme passion was a real turn on.

All of this is true. However, there is the other part of it, which doesn't reflect on the joy of the moment, but is greatly affected by it. Walking out of school and not having to face a teacher again also meant you would not graduate with your class and do the kinds of things you fancied afterward. Eating that gooey dessert meant you couldn't wear the outfit you were hoping to get into. Going to bed with someone in the height of passion meant an unwanted pregnancy, or some other disaster. It's not as simple as experiencing something in the moment. What you need to recognize is that you're conning yourself. Whenever you decide something has to be done right now, this very minute, see it as a con, and ask yourself what the consequences would be if you get caught. The used car you absolutely had to buy today with your family's vacation money might not work out to be as satisfying in the long run as in the short run.

Try to realize that you're conning yourself, you're fooling yourself, and you're playing games with yourself. At the very least, you're rationalizing.

Ask yourself at the moment you must have a dessert, "Am I going to get caught?" It's an interesting question, isn't it? From the moment you decide, you begin to rationalize. "It's really a small portion. I'll only eat the crust. I'll start dieting tomorrow. I was good yesterday. I only had a light lunch." I don't have to tell you all of the things you say to yourself.

If you ask yourself if you're going to get caught, you're response might be different. Yes, you're going to get caught. You're not going to lose the weight that you want to lose. Or, at the very least, you're not going to lose it quickly. Yes, you are always going to get caught.

Can you get caught quitting school? You need to think about it. Think of alternatives which are more desirable to you than going to school. Consider also the advantages to you in not quitting. If they outweigh the former, you can get caught.

The implications of having intercourse without preparation don't need much elaboration. Yes, you can get caught. And the same is true for the car versus the family vacation.

After realizing you can get caught, the next question to ask yourself is, "Is it worth it?" If the answer is "yes," enjoy the experience. If the answer is "no," and you decide either to delay or give up an experience that is only offered in the moment, you will also feel good about yourself. You will feel a sense of satisfaction, because you had a choice.

Having a choice is critical. It allows you the freedom to act or not to act, which is the greatest gift we can give ourselves. It frees you from the necessity of acing out your impulses, and puts you in charge of your life. What a very special place to be.

4

what about *your* children?

Children of alcoholics and children of children of alcoholics are no more, or no less, harmed emotionally than children living in any other kind of stressful situation. Alcoholism cannot claim exclusive rights to distressed children. The guilt that you carry because of your inability to provide an ideal home environment regardless of the circumstances will not do you a bit of good. It will not do your children a bit of good either. All it will do is take energy away from the things you could be doing to change the situation.

Much of the pain suffered by your children is reversible. Not only that, but with your help, your children can be stronger and have greater self-esteem because of their experiences. Yes, I mean that. Negatives can be turned into positives. It is all in knowing how. It has been my experience in counseling your children that improvement is immediate and dramatic. More often than not, enlisting your help is of great benefit in turning your child around. You are a significant person in your child's life and can be a strong force for well-being. There are many things that you can do that will enhance a sense of self-worth in your children.

WHAT ABOUT MY KIDS?

The following are some guidelines that will be useful to you in helping to break the cycle of problems caused by alcoholism in the next generation. There are ten very simple points.

Since many of you developed alcoholism yourselves, and many of you have married alcoholics, there is a good chance that your children are living in an active situation. The guidelines are developed with this in mind. If you are fortunate enough not to have become alcoholic yourself, and not living with it again, the guildelines will still be helpful. They can be adapted to any situation.

1. Work on yourself and your own personal growth.

Children learn through imitation. Be the kind of person you want your children to imitate. You are a role model—like it or not. You set the example. If you are upset and confused, your children will be upset and confused. If you are irritable, your children will be irritable. Your children became fearful and guilty and obsessed with alcohol, just as you did. Just as you can set a negative tone in the house, you can set a positive one. If you have a smile on your face, your children will smile. One can feel tension in the air. Not a word has to be spoken, but everybody feels it. If you can work on relaxing, the mood in your home will be more relaxed. It is a place to begin.

2. Listen to your children.

Sit down with them and hear what they have to say—regardless of what it is. Let them know that you are interested and that they have your attention. Because you listen does not mean you agree. It just means that you are willing to listen. Work on accepting their right to be who they are, and to think what they think, just as you want them to accept your right to be who you are and to think what you think. That is an easy thing to say, but it is a lot harder to do. Some of what you hear will be outrageous, but you had outrageous thoughts when you were that age too. Or even today. Because you listen without preaching does not mean you agree. It is simply a beginning of opening up the lines of communication. It is a beginning of talking to and not at.

3.   Tell the truth. Be honest with them.

Your children's sense of what is reality is badly distorted. They have difficulty in knowing the truth. The active alcoholic lies mostly in terms of broken promises. He means it when he says he will be home in time for dinner, even though this may not happen. This confuses children. The alcoholic is not lying, but does not get home in time for dinner. The child hears the non-alcoholic covering up and follows that example. The child also doesn't want to face the truth. No one does. But confronting reality is what will bring you back to health. Not having to hide feelings will ease the burden on your children.

Feelings are not RIGHT or WRONG. They just are. "You shouldn't feel that way," is not a helpful thing to hear or say, because we feel however we feel. Maybe there are certain ways we should not behave, but feelings have no right or wrong value. If we feel that what we are feeling is wrong, then we will feel guilty and it will make matters worse. Your child might say, "I hate my father!" For you to say, "You shouldn't hate your father, he is sick," is to lay guilt on the child. What a terrible person he must be to hate someone who is sick. It is better to explore the feelings with the child. "I know what you mean. Sometimes I think I hate him too, but it is really the disease that I hate. What I really hate is the way the disease makes him behave." Help to clarify. In so doing, you will help to clarify your own thinking.

The anger you feel is real. It is not helpful to decide that you are wrong to feel angry and should feel compassionate instead. You can feel both those things. Talk about it. Be open about it. Decide what you are going to do about it. Why not ride your bike if you're angry, or hit a punching bag, or find a place where you can scream to your heart's content? Yes, being angry is O.K. Behaving destructively because of the anger you feel is not O.K.

I am more concerned with the child who remains passive in a situation that I know he resents. I know that the anger the child turns inward will result in stomach problems, depression, and all sorts of other symptoms. If your children yell at you, as difficult as it is to take, it is healthier for them to get it out. Once it is out, you can sit down and talk about it. Children also worry a lot. They worry and they feel powerless. They are not comfortable confiding in their teachers and counselors. They don't want "outsiders" to know. So much of what concerns them is held inside. You can provide a haven. Worries, when talked about openly, seem more manageable.

4. **Educate them.**

Tell them everything you know about the disease of alcoholism. Give them literature and sit down with them and answer whatever questions they may ask. There may be some things they want to know that you cannot answer. "Yes, I understand that once Daddy starts to drink he can't stop, but why does he start?" And then you answer with, "He's so sick. The compulsion is a part of disease." And the child says, "Yes, but ..." At this point, there is nothing wrong with saying, "I don't fully understand it myself. The only answer I know for sure is that not letting it get us down is really hard work. I need your help to remember, just as you need my help to remember.

5.   Encourage your children to attend Alateen.

Alateen will help to reinforce the idea that alcoholism is a disease and must be looked at as such. Once your children can accept the disease concept, they can start to build their self-esteem. As children, we see ourselves as others see us. Those terrible things that the alcoholic says to the children affect the way they see themselves. Many times I have had children sobbing in my arms, "If I wasn't such a rotten kid, my parent wouldn't drink. Everybody would be better off if I were dead."

One cannot cause alcoholism, nor can one cure it. The child must understand that alcohol cannot be allowed to determine his value as a human being. This, again, is much easier said than done. You can help by constant reminding and by your own behavior toward your child.

Alateen is wonderful in reinforcing these ideas. If your child will attend Alateen, he will feel understood and have a sense of belonging. It is a place where he will be able to talk out his problems, and begin to feel better about himself.

6.   Give up denial.

Denial is the greatest ally that alcoholism has, and the biggest enemy that you who combat it have. Reality, however, is easier to deal with than the unknown. This is true, even with a disease as insidious as alcoholism. Say to your children: "Your daddy has an allergy to alcohol. It causes him to behave in ways that he does not want to, and we do not want him to, but we must not forget that when he acts those ways, it is the disease talking and not your daddy. That will be hard to remember, because he still looks like daddy. When you forget, come and talk to me about it, and when I forget I will come and talk to you. This is a family disease, and we will feel better as a family."

7. **Do not protect your children from knowing the ravages of alcoholism.**

If the alcoholic in your home destroys things, it is best for the alcoholic to see the evidence of the destruction. Unfortunately, the children may have to see it too. Say, "I feel bad that you have to see this, but Mommy must know what happened, or she will not remember." To protect your children is to make them weak and confused. They know something went on, so why leave it to their imagination? The imagination will make it far worse, no matter how bad it was. Reality cannot be denied. To spend energy denying what is real is to take that energy away from other things that can be more beneficial—like getting well.

8. **Don't be afraid to show affection to your children.**

There is no way that you can offer a child too much love. Giving in to his every whim to overcompensate for the difficulties of his life is not loving. To tell a child that you love him, to hold him, to kiss him, to let him know how lucky you feel that he is your kid, is loving. He needs to hear it. For you to say that he knows you love him is not enough, just as it is not enough for you. The child needs to hear it, as you need to hear it. This does not mean that everything he does and says is lovable. It just means that as a human being he is lovable. "I love who you are. I do not have to love all your behavior, and if I do not, I do not love you less." This message needs to be clear. You can love the alcoholic and hate the disease. One thing does not have anything to do with the other. Some behaviors are acceptable and some are not.

9. **It is important for children to have clearly defined limits.**

Let them know that dinner is served at a particular time, that going to bed and doing homework are scheduled. Give them parameters around which to order their lives. Their homelife needs to be consistent, for inconsistency so disorients children that they lose a sense of who they are. One cannot feel good about oneself if he doesn't know what is going on from day to day. It will throw him off balance. Offer him an ordered life with rules that are reasonable, and demand that these rules be followed. Children test limits, just to know if you really mean it. If the rule is fair, it does not matter whether or not the child likes it. Few do. But that does not mean that he will not be grateful for it, and feel more secure because of it. One must feel secure if one is to improve his sense of himself. You can help with this feeling.

10.   Children need to take responsibility for their behavior.
If your child breaks a window, it is his problem to figure out a way to replace it. His failures are his, and his successes are his. If he is late for dinner, it is his problem—not yours. Learning to manage difficulties is a part of building self-esteem. It means that he has some control over his environment. When your child has a problem, help him think through alternatives, but don't always supply him with the answer. Children of alcoholics feel helpless. Their lives are inflicted on them. They need help taking charge. Encourage them to try out new things. Succeeding is not as important as trying. Although one cannot fail if he does not try, one cannot succeed either. Any little success should be supported.

Think about the things that make you feel more worthy. Offer these same things to your children. Self-esteem does not change as one grows older without hard work. Work at it as a family. You suffered as a family—divided by alcoholism. Now recover as a family—united because of alcoholism.

Ironically enough, the terrible illness that has hit your family can be used against itself. Because of alcoholism, you became aware of yourself and your need to be a fully-functioning family. Take advantage of it. The power of self-growth—enhanced self-worth—renders alcoholism harmless. Your children will be stronger because they have dealt with reality. They will be less vulnerable because they have experienced the pain and faced it. We grow from the challenges in our lives. We grow from the hard times, not the easy ones. As a family, you can become more fulfilled than if you were never forced to face yourselves. Helping your children build their self-esteem will help you build yours. And building your self-esteem will help your children. This time, the spiral goes upward. Slowly, but surely, the pattern reverses itself and you are in the driver's seat—because YOU ARE WORTH IT!

CONCLUSION

There are three statements in the alcoholism field with which there appears to be agreement:

1. Alcoholism runs in families. Rarely do we see a case in isolation. Someone, somewhere else in the family usually has been, or is currently, suffering from the disease.
2. Children of alcoholics run a higher risk of developing alcoholism that children in the mainstream of the population. There may have been some discussion of environment or genetics, or a combination of both, but the truth of the statement is without question.
3. Children of alcoholics tend to marry alcoholics. They rarely go into the marriage with that knowledge, but we see this phenomenon occur over and over again.

These statements demonstrate the undeniable links between, and probably among, all aspects of the family disease we call alcoholism. The characteristics of the alcoholic and the family responses, as I point out in *Marriage on the Rocks*, clearly influence the variables that relate to the Adult Children of Alcoholics, as discussed in this book.

In *Marriage on the Rocks*, I talk about qualities that are prevalent among alcoholics, such as (a) excessive dependency; (b) inability to express emotions; (c) low frustration tolerance; (d) emotional immaturity; (e) high level of anxiety in interpersonal relationships; (f) low self-esteem; (g) grandiosity; (h) feelings of isolation; (i) perfectionism; (j) ambivalence toward authority; and (k) guilt.

The family responds with: (a) denial; (b) protectiveness, pity—concern about the drinker; (c) embarrassment, avoiding drinking occasions; (d) shift in relationship—domination, takeover, self-absorptive activities; (e) guilt; (f) obsession, continual worry; (g) fear; (h) lying; (i) false hope, disappointment, euphoria; (j) confusion; (k) sex problems; (l) anger; (m) lethargy, hopelessness, self-pity, remorse, despair.

In taking one last look at the characteristics that predominate with adult children of alcoholics, it is not hard to make linkages between these characteristics and what they experienced as children from both alcoholic and near-alcoholic parents. The qualities discussed as eminating from the alcoholic and the near-alcoholic contribute in part to each characteristic. You may want to add to or modify my list. Perceptions may vary, but regardless of the differences, the connections become obvious.

1. Adult children of alcoholics guess at what normal is.
    A—b,g,j; NA—aa, dd, hh, ii, jj
2. Adult children of alcoholics have difficulty following a project through from beginning to end.
    A—c,f,i; NA—ff, jj, mm
3. Adult children of alcoholics lie when it would be just as easy to tell the truth.
    A—g, i, j; NA—aa, ee, hh, ii, jj
4. Adult children of alcoholics judge themselves without mercy.
    A—i, j, k; NA—ee
5. Adult children of alcoholics have difficulty having fun.
    A—all; NA—all
6. Adult children of alcoholics take themselves very seriously.
    A—e, f, j, k; NA—all
7. Adult children of alcoholics have difficulty with intimate relationships.
    A—a, b, c, d, e, k; NA—aa, dd, jj, kk, ll
8. Adult children of alcoholics overreact to changes over which they have no control.
    A—c, i; NA—dd
9. Adult children of alcoholics constantly seek approval and affirmation.
    A—a, d, f, i, j; NA—ff, gg
10. Adult children of alcoholics usually feel different from other people.
    A—e, f, h; NA—cc, jj
11. Adult children of alcoholics are super responsible or super irresponsible.
    A—all; NA—all
12. Adult children of alcoholics are extremely loyal, even in the face of evidence that the loyalty is undeserved.
    A—a; NA—aa, bb, gg, ii
13. Adult children of alcoholics tend to lock themselves into a

course of action without giving serious consideration to alternative behaviors or possible consequences. This impulsivity leads to confusion, self-loathing, and loss of control of their environment. As a result, more energy is spent cleaning up the mess than would have been spent had the alternatives and consequences been examined in the first place.

A—c, d, g, j; NA—ii, jj, ll

Alcoholic.
a.   excessive dependency
b.   inability to express emotions
c.   low frustration tolerance
d.   emotional immaturity
e.   high level of anxiety in interpersonal relationships
f.   low self-esteem
g.   grandiosity
h.   feelings of isolation
i.   perfectionism
j.   ambivalence toward authority
k.   guilt

Near-Alcoholic.
aa.   denial
bb.   protectiveness, pity—concern about the drinker
cc.   embarrassment, avoiding drinking situations
dd.   shift in relationship—domination, takeover, self-absorptive activities
ee.   guilt
ff.   obsession, continual worry
gg.   fear
hh.   lying
ii.   false hope, disappointment, euphoria
jj.   confusion
kk.   sex problems
ll.   anger
mm.   lethargy, hopelessness, self-pity, remorse, despair

This demonstrates very clearly how adult children of alcoholic parents are the products of their environment. It is most fortunate that we know about the alcoholic home environment because it offers answers to questions that might otherwise not be understood. If knowledge is freeing, and I believe it is, knowing what happened and what can develop as a result is a very significant tool in understanding who you are and why. The guesswork goes out, the self-indictment loses its power, and you are free to work on what you chose. You are no longer a victim. You are in the center of your own universe. What a special place to be.

When you start to feel pulled, or driven, explore those feelings, don't judge them, and then let go of them in order to maintain your serenity and stay in the flow of your life.

The process of life is an adventure. Twisting, turning, going where it needs to go, and you with it right in the center, but letting it take its course. This is a peaceful and serene attitude, like that of Alcoholics Anonymous and the gifts of "Easy Does It," "One Day At A Time," and "Let Go and Let God."

Life is an ongoing process. If you are centered, if you are in control of your feelings, thoughts, and desires, you journey through life taking many little roads along the way, and experience each phase fully and completely. If you are in the center of your life, and not being pulled and swayed by your own impulses and by the desires of others, you will have a sense of serenity, a sense of real comfort within yourself.

That's what this book is all about. It offers the knowledge of where you were, and where you are. It puts today and tomorrow firmly in your hands. The choices are yours, whatever they may be. You are in charge of you, and that's all that really matters.

JANET WOITITZ ON ADULT CHILDREN OF ALCOHOLICS ISSUES

Best Seller!

BOOK TITLES

Ordering Instructions: